# TECH WRITING TIPS

## A PRACTICAL GUIDE FOR TECHNICAL PEOPLE

### A.M. EINSPRUCH

Cover design by 100 Covers.

Editing by Vanessa of Red Dot Scribble.

Proofreading by Abigail of Bothersome Words.

Layout by Andrew Einspruch of Wild Pure Heart.

ISBN: 978-0-6457981-0-4

# DEDICATION

*To my parents, Norman and Edith, and to my brothers, Eric and Franklin.*

*Thank you for your support.*

# CONTENTS

PART III
# TOOLS FOR BETTER WRITING

# THE PROMISE OF THIS BOOK

My technical writing career started in 1993. I responded to a newspaper classified ad (remember those?) by calling a consulting and placement agency that specialized in technical documentation. A guy named Phil answered the phone.

Phil (voice like Billy Connolly swallowing rocks): "So, you want to be a technical writer?"

Me (nervous, neutral Texan accent): "Well, uh, yes."

Phil: (Pause.) "You need to know something, mate."

Me: "Oh?"

Phil: "Technical writing is not for the faint-hearted."

And you know what?

Phil was right.

If you've ever tried to document a data structure, write up a software guide, file a bug report, draft a high-level system design, or summarize a system security architecture, then you'll know it can be hard.

And if you've ever had to read someone else's documented data structure, software guide, bug report, HLSD, or SSA, you'll know that lots of people aren't very good at it. One way or another, most technical documents are awful. Some of them are a little crummy, but others are absolutely horrific, their words strung together so badly you want to scream until your lungs explode, your life force siphoning away as if extracted by an alien beast birthed from the unholy marriage of passive voice, repetitive jargon, oDDly-FOrmed ACroNYMs, six-point fonts, and bad spelling.

But here's the thing. It's not that hard to make your documents better.

And that's the promise of this book.

I can help you make your documents less awful.

A *lot* less.

Writing is a bit like tennis. All of us can grab a racquet and have a go at whacking the ball over the net. With practice, a bit of coaching, and some persistence, we can all get better at it. We may never be as good as Serena Williams, but that's okay. We don't need to be. We just need to be able to hit the ball over the net consistently and with some degree of accuracy, and with any luck, tennis will turn into something that's actually fun.

"Hold it," you say. "Are you suggesting that writing technical documents might be fun?"

Of course not.

I'm not a monster.

But maybe we can get you to the point where you feel writing isn't torture; that it's something that you're capable of doing. You — yes, you — will be able to produce technical documents that are more accurate and easier to read. You'll achieve the writing equivalent of getting the ball over the net, consistently and clearly.

So, come on. Let's get to it.

# WHY WRITE WELL?

Obviously, *you're* not the kind of person who'd say, "My writing is terrible. So what? Who cares?"

How do I know that? Because you're reading this book.

But I do think it's worth taking a step back and looking at the value of well-written documentation.

Why write well?

I have four good reasons. (Obviously, there are more than four, but these'll do for now.)

First, it helps ensure that people will understand you. If your technical documents aren't clear and accurate, then the people using them are more likely to make errors and oopsies. If you're lucky, the boo-boo will be something small and no big deal.

But what if the thing you're documenting is mission-critical? You don't want your writing to lead to someone getting a call in the middle of the night asking why that red light is flashing, and by the way, are the servers supposed to belch out smoke like that?

Helping people avoid calls from the CIO is a great reason to have well-written documents.

Second, good documents help you build trust and credibility. Being able to clearly communicate gives people confidence that you know what you're talking about, and that they can rely on the information you provide.

Third, writing well saves the reader time. I'm sure you've had it happen to you: a badly-written document lands on your desk and you end up spending far too long trying to figure out what the person means. As you read, your frustration (and possibly your blood pressure) spikes because you have a To-Do list a thousand items long and you're wasting your time trying to decode this text.

Clear, effective communication is understood quickly and efficiently. This saves everyone time.

Last, well-written documentation helps people make good decisions. If management receives information that resembles the results of a cat dealing with a hairball, then it's hard for the reader to know what their options are, and the implications of each. You know the old adage about garbage in, garbage out, right? Hairball-like documentation leads to hairball-like decision-making.

And no one wants that.

Not even the cat.

# THE HATRED OF DOCUMENTING

*"The last thing a programmer wants to do is write documentation."*
—*Leo Laporte,* MacBreak Weekly[1]

H ave you ever met someone who writes code for a living?

Of course you have.

If you're reading this book, odds are that someone is you, or someone you work with.

If you've spent any time around coders, you'll know one thing for certain: they hate writing documentation.

We can generalize this: highly technical people, on the whole, hate writing documentation.

Why?

There are lots of reasons.

How many of these seem familiar?

- It takes time, which they don't have because of the deadline they're under.
- It's a hassle.
- They're not good at it, which makes it embarrassing when they're forced to do it.
- They don't know what to say.
- The system is going to change anyway, so why bother?
- English might not be their first language, so they feel writing is a challenge.
- They'd rather code than write documentation. It's more productive.
- They'd rather have their teeth extracted by a rabid weasel than write documentation. It's less painful.
- Writing documentation is boring.
- Hey, can't you just read the code? It's all in there.
- Their minds don't work that way. They're good at thinking the way you have to think to get a computer sit up and do tricks. But explaining those tricks to a human? That's just not how they're wired.

This aversion to documentation is, of course, not solely the domain of coders and highly technical people. Lots of other folks hate it, too. You can tell just by reading what they write.

But it seems particularly acute in technical folks.

And yet...

It has to be done.

If you don't document that application or system, someone, sooner or later, is going to be in a world of hurt. All CIOs know that the road to hell is paved with a lack of documentation. (And we know that CIOs tend not to keep their hell to themselves. They share it around.) Even if you were the person who wrote the code, the person in a world of hurt could well be you. If you have to fix something you coded half a year ago (or three years ago), documentation can help with that.

Ideally, the organization you work for hires technical writers to offload the documentation burden. But probably they don't, or not enough of them. So it's on you to do it.

Don't worry. You got this. Just apply what's in these pages and you'll be fine.

~

**The Two Parts to Writing Well**

There are two parts to writing well — getting the thoughts and ideas right, and getting the words right.

This book is divided up along those lines.

Part One is a short section designed to help you identify the thoughts you're trying to convey.

Part Two is full of tips to help you get the words right, so you can convey those thoughts well.

There's also a Part Three, which covers tools for better writing.

# PART I

## GETTING THE THOUGHTS RIGHT

# 1

## THE TWO MOST IMPORTANT QUESTIONS

There are two questions I always ask when I agree to write a document:

- Who's the audience for it? (In other words, who's going to read it?)
- What do they need to know to do their job?

Knowing who your audience is makes all the difference. Are you writing a summary report for your branch head? Are you trying to convey some technical quirk to your manual testers? Who you are talking to matters. The information needs of your CIO or CEO are very different to those of your sysadmins, even if what you're writing about is the same.

So Question One is *always*, "Who's the audience?"

It's a simple question. But in practice, defining your audience can be hard to do. It's a more complex process than perhaps it appears at first blush.

Here's a short list of questions that can help define the audience:

- What's their level of expertise?
- What's their level of education?
- What are their goals?
- What are their interests?
- How familiar are they with your topic?
- And here's a big one: what can you consider assumed knowledge, and what do you need to spell out?

Once you've worked *who* your audience is, then you need to think about *what* they need to know. I normally phrase this as "What do they need to know to do their job?" because that helps me focus on what's important. Even if there's a lot of detail in whatever it is you're writing about, the audience might only need a little bit of it to get the job done. It also helps you work out how much technical detail to include.

People in management tend to want bigger picture stuff, like how long the system has been down, how many Severity 1 bugs are in the defect queue, or total throughput per hour of the system. Those working hands-on with the system itself are more likely to understand (and to need) the nitty-gritty detail, like which system-specific sub-routine is crashing, or the exact error code generated by the fault.

These two questions apply whether you're sending an email, doing an annual report, or submitting a system security design to the Architecture Board.

What if your document has a wide audience? No problem, this happens all the time. In that case, your document can have both high-level information for management as well as the detail the more hands-on staff need. Just organize it so that the former can find what they need at a glance (perhaps by including an executive summary up front), and it's easily understood by the latter.

So, let me say it again. Always start with:

- Who's your audience?
- What do they need to know to do their job?

∾

**The Other Two Questions**

Once I've answered the two questions I talked about above, I ask Questions Three and Four.

The third is, "When do you need this done by?"

Inevitably, I have a stack of things to do, so I need to know if this is a "hair on fire" document that the CIO wants *right now* or a "when you can get around to it" task from the guy three cubicles over who needs it sometime in the next month[1].

The fourth question is, "Who's going to pay for this?"

Is it project-funded? Is it supposed to be a business as usual (BAU) cost? Asking this question up front ensures no one is surprised later on when you start looking for a cost code to put in the time-tracking system.

∾

**Exercise: Answering the Two Questions**

Think about a document you need to write or that you've written recently, and ask yourself those two questions:

- Who's your audience?
- What do they need to know to do their job?

Take a moment to actually write your answers down. Express in words who you think the audience is and what they need to know.

Now do the same exercise, but this time for an email that you need to write. If you're not sure what to do, then assume the email is meant to convince someone to buy a particular piece of equipment, or explain the cause of a system outage.

And then do this exercise for another document that's relevant to you.

The point is to try asking these questions about different kinds of documents, to see how they apply in different contexts.

If you're coming up blank for this exercise, then try one of these ideas as the basis of an email:

- What to do for this year's holiday party.
- The refrigerator is being cleaned on Friday.
- The organization is instituting a One Computing Device Per Person Policy.

There are sample answers for each of these in the *Appendix: Exercise Answers*.

**2**
---

# WHAT I'M TRYING TO SAY IS...

When you're writing, it's important to remember that what you want to say is different to *how* you need to say it. They're related, but different. You need to get the "what" clear in your head before the "how."

Why "what" before "how?"

It's like creating a PowerPoint or Keynote presentation. When you start your slide deck, you have to resist the temptation to immediately decide on the colors, the fancy graphics, and whether you can get away with including a cartoon. This all comes later.

Before any of that, you need to figure out *what you want to say.*

What if you're not sure what it is you're trying to communicate?

Try this:

1. Look away from your screen or whatever you're writing on.
2. Out loud, say, "What I'm trying to say is..."
3. Say whatever it is that you're trying to say.
4. Write down those thoughts.

Don't worry about how pretty the words are, just get them out. "What I'm trying to say is..." clarifies your intent and helps you get to the core of your message. Don't worry about the elegance of it or the grammar or spelling. Just spew it out and write it down.

For example:

> What I'm trying to say is that we need to come up with an approach to performance testing that is less likely to cause a time crunch just before release because the environment is unstable or the developers and manual testers are late because they've found defects. Probably, we need to do some sort of interim performance testing (is this possible with the current setup of environments?). Or we need to go ahead and take the plunge and adopt Agile so we can do performance testing as we go, rather trying to do it all at the end.

You see how I haven't worried about the way I've expressed the ideas? I'm just trying to get them down.

Once you've done that, look at what you've got, and ask yourself, "Is that really what I want to say?"

If so, great.

If not, try again, or make changes to the version you've already got.

Once you have the ideas right, *then* you can work out how best to express them.

∾

### Idea Dots and Mind Maps

There are other ways to get your ideas down. Instead of saying the "What I'm trying to say..." phrase out loud, you can do it on paper. This might be in the form of mind-mapping, outlining, or (my personal favorite) listing your ideas as dot points.

Don't worry about the order or the word choice, just get the thoughts down. Later, you can reorder and refine them. Maybe things will stay as a dot list, or maybe they'll be expanded into a paragraph. That's for later. First, the ideas.

Here's the example from above done as dot points.

*Performance testing:*

- *Too often a time crunch.*
- *Performance testing usually pushed to the end of release.*
- *Unstable environments cause problems.*
- *Devs and tests get late when defects are found.*
- *Late updates squeeze performance testing window at end of release cycle.*
- *Solution (a): interim performance testing. (Do we need to spin up another environment?)*
- *Solution (b): take the plunge and go Agile. This would let us incorporate performance testing as we go.*

It isn't pretty, but it gets the job done. Now that the ideas have been teased out, they can be worked with.

If you were mind-mapping, it might look something like this:

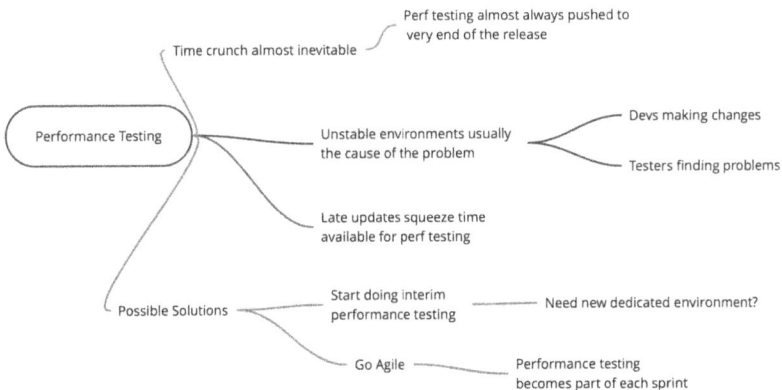

You get the idea. Use whatever tool helps you get the ideas out of your head and onto the page.

~

**Exercise: What I'm Trying to Say**

Use one of the methods shown in this chapter (text, dot points, or mind map) to figure out what you want to say in a document or email.

If you don't have a document in mind, go back to the suggestions from the previous chapter:

- What to do for this year's holiday party.
- The refrigerator is being cleaned on Friday.
- The organization is instituting a One Computing Device Per Person Policy.

In the previous chapter, the exercise was about who the audience is, and what they need to know.

Here, you'll map out the things you want to say.

I've done a sample answer for each of these, which you'll find in the *Appendix: Exercise Answers*.

~

**Now That We Know What We're Trying to Say**

To recap, you've used the exercises outlined above to articulate the points you want to make.

So, now that you know what you want to say, let's turn our attention to saying it well.

It's time for Part Two: Getting the Words Right.

# PART II

## GETTING THE WORDS RIGHT

# 3

## MY ONE BIG WRITING TIP

If you take nothing else from this book, I hope you come away with this:

*Give yourself permission to write the worst garbage in the world.*

I mean that literally. It's one of the biggest tips I have to offer.

Allow yourself to barf out the worst writing that has ever splattered onto a piece of paper or polluted a computer's memory. Give yourself the freedom to spew the writing equivalent of slime. Make it okay to emit the most execrable words to grace the face of the earth since the first person put quill to papyrus.

You need to let yourself do that.

Spelling mistakes, grammar goofs, run-on sentences, bad word choices, sentence fragments, the verbal equivalent of throat clearing — anything goes.

Why?

Two reasons.

First, it may take you a few paragraphs or a few pages of verbal nonsense to get to the core nugget of an idea. If you don't give yourself permission to write badly, that nugget will stay locked in your head, because you're too focused on perfecting your words, which cuts off the flow of your thoughts. Writing freely without judgement makes it more likely you'll enter a flow state where the ideas you need are allowed to emerge.

Second: *writing is rewriting.*

There's no getting around it: you will eventually have to revise what you've written. The longer the document, the truer this is. But you can't revise a blank page. You have to start somewhere. So don't get hung up on whether your writing is any good. Allow it to be appalling. Once you have something to work with, you can revise it.

Professional writers know all about this trick. Hollywood screenwriters will often refer to the first draft of their screenplay as the "vomit draft." They just have to get the ideas out, then they can start polishing them.

So, let me say it again. Give yourself permission to write the worst garbage in the world.

It's very freeing, and a great place to start.

$\sim$

**Exercise: Writing Whatever**

Let's write some garbage.

1. Set a timer for three minutes.
2. Get a pen and paper (writing on paper works better for this exercise than using your computer, because it's much easier to wad up and burn a piece of paper).
3. Write anything you like, as fast as you can, for three minutes.

Don't know what to write about? Try one of these prompts:

- Please, please marry my son.
- Dawn rose like a whip crack.
- Edward found true happiness in the condiments aisle.

It really doesn't matter what you write, just give yourself permission to write without hesitation.

Bonus exercise: try doing this with a document you need to write. Just start writing and see what happens. Write as fast as you can for, say, five minutes, and just let the words flow. You might just be amazed at how much this can help.

# 4

## ADAPTING TO AUDIENCES

I n the chapter *The Two Most Important Questions*, I explained that you have to know who your audience is to write well for them.

This, by extension, means that you need to adapt your writing to meet the needs of that audience.

But how, exactly, do you do that? How do you tailor your writing to meet the needs of your audience?

Good question.

You have a number of tools at your disposal, including:

- word choice
- assumed knowledge
- document purpose
- examples
- analogies
- visuals.

Let's look at each of these.

**Word Choice**

As we'll discuss in the chapter *Fewer Words, Shorter Words*, I'm a fan of brevity. I try to say things with fewer, shorter words. So, that's my starting point.

With this in mind, knowing your audience helps you tailor your word choice to suit their level of technical understanding, education, and experience. If you're writing a quick-start guide for people who have never touched a computer before, your writing will be very different than if your audience haa a solid understanding of computers and their use.

As a rule, the more general the audience, the more basic you want the language to be (sometimes to the point of avoiding technical language entirely). For a more specialized audience, you can ramp up the level of technical language to match their understanding.

**Assumed Knowledge**

Here's an example of assumed knowledge:

*Splunk.*

Is that a sound effect?

Or is it software used for searching, monitoring, and analyzing machine-generated data, like log files?

If I'm writing a technical doc, do I need to explain "Splunk" or not?

Say it with me: *it depends on the audience.*

Knowing your audience helps you determine what knowledge can be assumed, and what can't be. If I'm writing a troubleshooting standard operating procedure (SOP) for a team of performance analysts at a DevOps shop, I can safely assume they know Splunk isn't a sound effect, even if they don't use the software themselves. But if I'm writing an introductory guide to performance analysis for recent university graduates, I probably need to explain what Splunk is and, broadly, how and why it's used.

In general, the more technical the audience, the more prior knowledge you can assume.

However, this is tempered by the fact that, especially with technical audiences, your assumed knowledge may be very domain-specific. They may be all over Splunk, but have no idea about Jira or Confluence or NeoLoad or [insert your tool of choice]. Keeping your audience in mind helps you assume knowledge appropriately.

### Document Purpose

The purpose of your document affects the way you write it. For example, if you're writing a user manual with the purpose of describing how a piece of software works, it will need to be very detailed, precise, and clear, and will probably have a lot of step-by-step instructions.

A research paper with the purpose of describing a scientific finding might involve more complex language and include more technical minutia.

A quick-start guide with the purpose of getting a user up and running as fast as possible will focus on essential steps, and be as brief as is practical.

### Examples

Knowing your audience lets you choose examples that are meaningful to them. For instance, take this sentence that appeared in the first chapter:

> *If you've ever tried to document a data structure, write up a software guide, file a bug report, draft a high-level system design, or summarize a system security architecture, then you'll know it can be hard.*

I know the people reading this are likely technically savvy and probably involved in information technology (IT). In that sentence, I specifically chose examples those readers can understand and relate to. If I was writing a book for doctors, my examples would be very different.

> *If you've ever tried to replace a heart valve, remove tonsils, clean up after a burst appendix, reconstruct a nose, or suture closed a knife wound, you'll know that surgery can be hard.*

See what I mean? Your choice of examples helps tailor your text to your audience.

## Analogies

An analogy is where you compare two different things to explain or clarify a complex idea by relating them. Analogies help you make abstract ideas more concrete, and easier to understand.

Here's an example:

> *A computer network is like a hotel with connected rooms, where each room is a computer, and each room number is an IP address.*

In this analogy, I'm comparing a computer network to a hotel to help readers understand how a computer network functions. Of course, the analogy only goes so far, but it can help offer clarity.

Appropriate analogies help you match your text to your audience.

For more on this, see the chapter *Similes, Metaphors, and Analogies*.

## Visuals

You know how they say a picture is worth a thousand words?

That's bulldust.

I've done the math, and a picture is worth exactly 923 words.

Okay, I'm kidding. But I don't entirely agree with the saying. I'd say that the right picture with the right information presented in the right way is worth a thousand words. It's all well and good to include an infographic, but it's only helpful if there's useful info in that graphic.

Diagrams, tables, charts, and graphs are all ways to organize information so that it is easier to understand. And they're all tools for tailoring your document to your audience. The complexity, style, and colors used in these visuals can all help your audience understand what you're trying to say.

So think about what visuals will help your audience comprehend your message. Do you need to represent something concrete or an abstract idea? Do they need a screen shot? A schematic? A workflow diagram? Are you conveying data? If so, what bigger idea does that data represent?

These sorts of questions help you decide what visual is most appropriate. And taken more broadly, they help guide whether you need a visual at all, or one of the other tools discussed in this chapter.

# 5

## ACTIVE VOICE

I f there's a plague in technical and business documents, that disease's name is "passive voice."

But there's an antidote — it's "active voice."

Active voice is when you construct your sentences so that their subject is performing the action directly. For example:

*The sysadmin performed yet another miracle.*

Here, the subject (noun) is "sysadmin," the action (verb) is "performed," and the target is "miracle." So we have a sentence that's constructed with the pattern *subject + action + target*.

*Sysadmin + performed + miracle.*

*subject + action + target*

Passive voice flips this around. It uses the format *target + action + subject*. Our example above, expressed in passive voice, would read:

*Yet another miracle was performed by the sysadmin.*

Broken down, that's:

*Miracle + was performed + sysadmin*

*target + action + subject*

The superpower for spotting passive sentences is looking for some form of the verb "to be." They're always there — typically "was," "has been," or "is" — used with the main verb.[1]

Here's a sample text. Have a read and see if you can spot the passive constructions.

*A series of tests were carried out by the Performance Testing Team. A large number of unexpected Sev 1 defects were found, causing the release to be postponed by the project manager for four months. Measurable financial losses will be suffered by the Department. The price is estimated by the Finance Team at $1.4 million, but it could be more.*

Do you see the passives there? "Were carried." "Were found." "To be postponed." "Will be suffered." "Is estimated."

When I'm given a document to edit, flipping passives to actives are quick writing wins. How would you do that with the paragraph above? Take a minute to try rewriting it, then have a look at my version, here:

*The Performance Testing Team carried out a series of tests. They found a large number of unexpected Sev 1 defects, causing the project manager to postpone the release for four months. The Department will suffer measurable financial losses. The Finance Team estimates the price at $1.4 million, but it could be more.*

Can you see how the rewrite is more direct and punchier? It's also more succinct, using eight fewer words (that's 13.3%).

Am I saying you should never use passive sentences? Of course not. Plenty of them can be found in this book. (That was one right there!) There's a time and a place for passive voice, even if usually you want to go active.

One good use of passives is when you're trying to obscure. You see politicians do this all the time.

*"Campaign financing laws have been broken."*

*"Mistakes were made."*

*"The contract was awarded fraudulently."*

*"Bribes were taken."*

There's an implied "it's not my fault" built into those statements. Compare the above to their active counterparts:

*"I broke campaign financing laws."*

*"We made mistakes."*

*"My team awarded the contract fraudulently."*

*"I took a bribe."*

The passive form of the sentences obscures who performed the action.

To repeat, I'm not saying all passive sentences are bad. But getting rid of them is crucial to stronger, clearer writing.

Where possible, ~~active voice should be used~~ use active voice.

**Exercise: Rewriting in Active Voice**

Here's a list of sentences written in passive voice. Try rewriting them in active voice. You'll find my versions in the *Appendix: Exercise Answers*.

1. The data will be encrypted by the server before it is transmitted to the client.
2. The application is being developed by the team using the latest software development methodologies.
3. The issue was fixed by the developer after several hours of debugging and troubleshooting.
4. The proposal will be reviewed by the project manager before it is presented to the stakeholders.
5. The system was audited by the compliance team to ensure it meets the regulatory requirements.
6. The data will be analyzed by the data scientist using machine learning algorithms to identify patterns and trends.
7. The network is being monitored by the security team to detect and prevent unauthorized access and attacks.
8. The algorithm was optimized by the researcher to reduce the computational complexity and improve the accuracy of the predictions.
9. The update is being tested by the QA team to ensure it does not introduce new bugs or issues.
10. The report is being generated by the software and will be sent to the stakeholders for review and feedback.
11. The project was completed by the team on time and on budget.
12. The requirements will be gathered by the business analyst and documented in the project plan.
13. The system failure is being investigated by the support team to determine the root cause and find a solution.
14. The data will be backed up by the cron job at regular intervals to prevent data loss.

15. The application update was deployed by the operations team using automated deployment scripts and configurations.
16. The system will be upgraded by the IT team to version 6.3.1 of the operating system for improved security and performance.
17. The code is being reviewed by the senior developer to ensure it meets the coding standards and best practices.
18. The feature will be implemented by the developer in the next software release.
19. The object is instantiated by the constructor method and initialized with default values before being modified by the program logic.
20. The exception was caught by the try-catch block and handled by the error management code to prevent a system crash.

# 6

## FEWER WORDS, SHORTER WORDS

On August 9, 1940, Winston Churchill had a fair bit happening. He'd only been prime minister for three months, and already he'd had to deal with the retreat at Dunkirk, the fall of Paris, and the conquest of France. The Battle of Britain would start four days later, and the Blitz bombings were only a month away.

You know what Churchill didn't have time for?

Long-winded briefs.

Mr Churchill knew a thing or two about writing. He was later awarded a Nobel Prize for Literature, and as prime minister, he sent and received thousands of memos and briefs.

On August 9, when he was right in the thick of things, he put out a short memo to his advisors called "Brevity."

Here's how it started:

*To do our work, we all have to read a mass of papers. Nearly all of them are far too long. This wastes time, while energy has to be spent in looking for the essential points.*

The memo lists four points where he wanted improvement. Here's the fourth:

*(iv) Let us have an end of such phrases as these: "It is also of importance to bear in mind the following considerations...", or "Consideration should be given to the possibility of carrying into effect...". Most of these woolly phrases are mere padding, which can be left out altogether, or replaced by a single word. Let us not shrink from using the short expressive phrase, even if it is conversational.*

Winston was totally right about woolly phrases and padding.

Want a simple way to improve your readability and clarity?

Embrace the following two rules:

*Use fewer words.*
*Use shorter words.*

For technical writing especially, I'm a big fan of short and sweet. If I can say something in a tech document with shorter and fewer words, I will.

- I'll "start," not "commence." (That's one syllable vs. two).
- Alternatively, I'll "begin" instead of "commence." (Fewer letters, even if it is the same number of syllables).
- I'll use "currently" not "at this point in time."
- "In order to" can always have the "in order" bit chopped off, leaving just "to."
- "Is able to" does not work as well as "can."
- "Is reliant upon" becomes "Relies on."

I literally count syllables to use fewer of them.

"What's the point?" you might ask. "What's an extra syllable here and there?"

Over the sentences, paragraphs, and pages, they add up.

Like Churchill, your audience doesn't have time to waste looking for the essential points.

But more, this kind of tightening helps make your text more accessible and engaging. That's because it removes jargon, complex words, and words that look like the writer is just trying to show off. By trimming back this way, you are less likely to come off as pompous or off-putting.

Shorter and simpler is almost always clearer. Your goal is to get people to understand what you're telling them, not to impress them with how grandiloquent you are. I say, trade fancy speakin' for plain speakin'.

Let's explore an example. Try simplifying this:

> *The updating of the work from home agreements for the next financial year was commenced by the team this past week.*

Let's look at changes we could make:

- "This past week" could become "Last week," saving a word.
- "Was commenced by the team" is better as "the team started." It is two words and two syllables shorter. More importantly, the sentence now uses active voice (see the previous chapter).
- Putting the sentence in active voice means I can trade "The updating of," where "updating" is used as a noun, for "updating," used as a verb. Swapping a noun construction for a verb is a very handy trick.

- If it is clear from the surrounding sentences that we're talking about the next financial year, or if everyone knows the work from home agreements cover a financial year, then I could drop the word "financial," and just have "next year." If this can't be assumed, I might use "fiscal" instead of "financial," as it is shorter.
- I could make "next year" a possessive of "work from home agreements," so this reads "next year's work from home agreements." This eliminates "for the."

Put the above tweaks together, and you have:

> *Last week, the team started updating next year's Work From Home agreements.*

That version of the sentence is a lot sharper and more to the point.

Obviously, I can't list every word and phrase that can possibly be simplified or improved, but below are numerous examples of the kind of changes you can make. Note that some of these are preferences, rather than actual simplifications, because I think they're more accessible to the reader ("after" instead of "post," and "affects" rather than "impacts"). Still, I consider each of these an improvement.

Have a go for yourself. Look at my examples below and see if you can say the same thing using fewer and/or shorter words.

**Don't Use This ⇒ Use This Instead**

**At this point in time ⇒ Currently**

*At this point in time, we have no clues.*

Currently, we have no clues.

**Utilize ⇒ Use**

*The testers utilize the automatic testing framework.*

The testers use the automatic testing framework.

**In order to ⇒ To**

*In order to improve response times, we plugged in the computer.*

To improve response times, we plugged in the computer.

**Functionality ⇒ Function**

*The software upgrade has an improved design and new functionality.*

The software upgrade has an improved design and new functions.

**Is able to ⇒ Can**

*Management is able to contain costs.*

Management can contain costs.

**Has the potential to ⇒ Could**

*The new system has the potential to change customer behavior.*

The new system could change customer behavior.

**Are reliant on ⇒ Rely on**

*Our cost projections are reliant on data supplied by the Asset Management Team.*

Our cost projects rely on data supplied by the Asset Management Team.

**Due to the fact that ⇒ Because**

*The server room filled with smoke due to the fact that there was an electrical fault.*

The server room filled with smoke because there was an electrical fault.

**Prior to ⇒ Before**

*Prior to go-live, the team must resolve all defects.*

Before go-live, the team must resolve all defects.

## Impacts ⇒ Affects

*The release impacts all related systems.*

The release affects all related systems.

## Post ⇒ After

*We'll debrief post release.*

We'll debrief after the release.

(Note that this one goes against the fewer words guidance, as well as the fewer syllables rule. However, it is easier to understand and less awkward.)

## Can be [verb] ⇒ Are [verb]

*Paper towels can be found in the cabinet.*

Paper towels are found in the cabinet.

(Better yet, make it active instead of passive, "You'll find paper towels in the cabinet." Also good: "Paper towels are in the cabinet.")

## Indicated ⇒ Showed

*The CIO indicated interest in the software system.*

The CIO showed interest in the software system.

## The manner in which ⇒ How

*The manner in which this problem is resolved will affect all future development.*

How this problem is resolved will affect all future development.

## Comprises ⇒ Has

*The committee comprises a chairperson, a vice chairperson, and seven ordinary members.*

The committee has a chairperson, a vice chairperson, and seven ordinary members.

**Regarding (or With regard to)** ⇢ **About**

*I'm writing with regard to our previous discussion.*

I'm writing about our previous discussion.

**A greater level of** ⇢ **More**

*We're seeing a greater level of defects.*

We're seeing more defects.

**Refer to** ⇢ **See**

*For more information, refer to Appendix A.*

For more information, see Appendix A.

**Contains a list** ⇢ **Lists**

*The following table contains a list of common terms.*

The following table lists common terms.

**Per annum** ⇢ **Per year**

*The license costs $100 per annum.*

The license costs $100 per year.

**Usage** ⇢ **Use**

*The app is in common usage within the Department.*

The app is in common use within the Department.

**Whilst** ⇢ **While**

*The upgrade will occur whilst the system is in maintenance mode.*

The upgrade will occur while the system is in maintenance mode.

**In excess of ⇒ More than**

*There are in excess of 500 candidates for the role.*

There are more than 500 candidates for the role.

**Terminates or Aborts ⇒ Ends**

*The process terminates when an error is thrown.*

*The process aborts when an error is thrown.*

The process ends when an error is thrown.

**In the event of ⇒ If**

*In the event of rain, the company picnic will be moved to the servicemen's club.*

If it rains, the company picnic will move to the servicemen's club.

**Should you wish to ⇒ If you want to**

*Should you wish to proceed, please send us a return email as confirmation.*

If you want to proceed, please email a confirmation.

**Particulars ⇒ Details**

*The software's particulars can be found in the brochure.*

The software's details are in the brochure.

∽

HAVING A LIST LIKE THE ONE ABOVE IS A GOOD EXERCISE. TRY MAKING your own list of simplifications and improvements, then refer to it when you write.

∽

## Generative AI Tools

I talk about ChatGPT and similar tools in the chapter *ChatGPT and Generative AI*. However, I'll mention here that this kind of simplification is something those tools can do well. You can give the tool a paragraph of text and ask it to rewrite it with fewer, shorter words while maintaining the meaning, and it will do a credible — even very good — job. Give it a try. (Just make sure you don't upload anything commercial-in-confidence or classified.)

~

## Exercise: Rewrite to Make More Concise

Rewrite the following sample paragraphs to use fewer, shorter words while conveying the same meaning. You'll find my take on the rewrites in the *Appendix: Exercise Answers*.

### Sample 1

The utilization of multiple, distinct components in a computer system can result in increased processing capacity and improved performance. This is due to the fact that when these components are integrated, their individual functionalities can be leveraged in a complementary manner, resulting in a more efficient and effective system overall. This is particularly important in complex computing environments, where a single component may not be capable of handling all of the required tasks on its own.

### Sample 2

When designing software applications, it is important to take into consideration a variety of factors that can impact performance and usability. This includes factors such as the user interface design, the programming language utilized, the underlying architecture of the application, and the hardware resources available. By carefully considering these factors, developers can create software that is both efficient and user-friendly.

## Sample 3

The rapid advancement of technology has led to the development of increasingly sophisticated tools and techniques for data analysis. These tools are designed to help organizations make sense of large and complex datasets, allowing them to extract valuable insights and inform decision-making processes. By leveraging these tools, organizations can gain a competitive advantage in their respective industries and stay ahead of the curve.

## Sample 4

The adoption of cloud computing has become increasingly popular in recent years, as organizations seek to leverage the scalability and flexibility offered by cloud-based services. Cloud computing enables organizations to access computing resources on demand, rather than having to invest in and maintain their own infrastructure. This can lead to significant cost savings, as well as increased agility and responsiveness.

## Sample 5

In order to protect sensitive data and ensure the security of computing systems, it is necessary to implement robust security protocols and procedures. This includes measures such as encryption, access controls, and regular system patching and updates to address known vulnerabilities. By taking a proactive approach to security, organizations can mitigate the risk of cyber attacks and protect themselves from potential threats.

# 7

# CONCRETE AND SPECIFIC

One key to effective writing is using language that's concrete and specific. This decreases the likelihood that your readers will misunderstand what you've said. Being concrete and specific shows you know what you're talking about, and can be precise about your topic.

"Concrete" language is where you refer to things that are tangible and observable. If I say, "The chair is carved from maple," I'm being concrete because the fact that the chair is made from wood, and in particular, from maple, is something that can be observed.

"Specific" language is defined, precise, and has a clear meaning. The sentence, "The Cisco UCS C240 M6 Rack Server has up to two 3rd Gen Intel Xeon Scalable processors with up to 40 cores per socket," is super specific. It says exactly which model server I'm talking about, and exactly which processors and cores can be configured.

Concrete and specific go hand-in-hand, and there's often a lot of overlap between the two, so don't worry too much about making the distinction.

Let's look at some examples of vague language versus concrete and specific language.

∽

Vague ⇒ Concrete and Specific

*The laptop has a large storage capacity.*

The laptop has 512 gigabytes of RAM and four terabytes of SSD storage.

*The program is easy to use.*

The program has a user-friendly interface with clearly labeled buttons and intuitive navigation. It complies with the Web Content Accessibility Guidelines (WCAG) 2.2 guidelines.

*The algorithm is more efficient.*

The algorithm completes the task in an average of 0.25 seconds, which is 60% faster than the previous release.

*The laptop's display is high resolution.*

The laptop's display is 13.3-inches (measured diagonally). It's an LED-backlit panel with 2,560 × 1,600 native resolution at 227 pixels per inch, and can display up to 500 nits of brightness.

*The system is fast.*

The system processes up to two terabytes of data per hour with up to one billion calculations per second.

*The system is secure.*

The system uses AES-256 encryption, and all users must log in with two-factor authentication using a hardware fob.

*The device is energy efficient.*

The devices consumes no more than 100 watts per hour, which is half the energy used by the previous model.

~

You see what I mean? The second of each pair is much clearer in what it's saying. The examples are concrete and specific.

"Hold on," you say. "A chapter ago, you pontificated about using fewer words and shorter words."

First of all, it wasn't pontification. It was solid writing advice.

But yes, I did.

"Aren't you contradicting yourself?"

Yes and no.

Yes, I've added a bunch of words, some of them lengthy, breaking both the fewer and shorter rules.

But, depending on the audience, it might just be what they need.

Ask this: what's our goal?

It's to communicate clearly.

Brevity is part of clarity (as our friend Mr Churchill preached). But clarity also comes from providing enough detail to give your reader the facts they need. Concrete, specific details that are relevant to your audience are key to ensuring your message is clear. Especially in technical documents, those details can make all the difference. So include them.

~

**Exercise: Rewrite to Make More Concrete and Specific**

The following sentences are vague and wishy-washy. Rewrite them to make them concrete and specific. My takes are in the *Appendix: Exercise Answers.*

1. The software features a user-friendly interface.
2. The mobile phone has a long battery life.
3. The server handles a large number of simultaneous requests.
4. The programming language is efficient.
5. The algorithm processes data quickly.
6. The API has a broad range of functionalities.
7. The security software protects against numerous threats.
8. The mobile app has many useful features.
9. The database stores a significant amount of information and keeps it safe.
10. The project management tool is versatile.

# 8

## STRUCTURE IS YOUR FRIEND

L et's assume that we know who our audience is, what kind of document we're writing, and the document's purpose. All of these things help us figure out what kind of structure our document should have.

This is important, because a clear structure helps readers understand the information we're giving them. It also helps us plan what we need to include.

For some reports, there may be templates already set up for you to use, which is handy. If you do a Performance Test Summary Report once per release, and there are three releases per year, there's no point in reinventing that particular wheel each time.

But if you don't have a template to follow, you'll need to think about your structure.

The most basic document structure is one you probably encountered in high school:

- **Introduction.** Introduces your subject, gives the background for why you're writing about it, and sets out expectations so your reader knows your purpose. This section sets up the rest of your document.

- **Body.** This is where all your main points go, along with your supporting information. If the document is longer than a page or two, you'll want to use headings and sub-headings, and maybe even sections and sub-sections to organize everything. (See the chapter *Headings, Tables, Lists, and Formatting* for details.)
- **Conclusion.** Here, you summarize your main points, highlight key takeaways, and spell out any implications. If there are next steps recommended, they go here too.

That's nice and general.

But it won't meet the needs, say, of a system security architecture, a software manual, or a business policy.

Take the software manual. It might look like this:

- **Introduction.** An overview of the software and its features, system requirements, and installation instructions.
- **Getting Started.** How to set up and configure the software.
- **User Interface.** How the user interface works, covering menus, buttons, and icons, and what they do.
- **Features and Functions.** This is the main how-to section, covering the bulk of what the program does.
- **Tips and Tricks.** Suggestions that help users work more efficiently.
- **Troubleshooting.** Solutions to common problems, with error messages and steps for solving specific problems.
- **Customizations.** How to customize the software to meet specific needs, such as specific look-and-feel options, accessibility options, or custom templates.
- **Glossary.** Definitions for any technical terms used.

Obviously, the structure will vary from company to company and app to app, but you get the idea.

A system architecture might look like this:

- **Introduction.** An overview of the project, including the problem the system addresses, its goals and objectives, and the project's scope.
- **Requirements.** Defines the functional and non-functional system requirements, including performance, security, and usability requirements.
- **Architecture.** Gives an overview of the system's high-level architecture, including system components, their relationships, and the overall system structure.
- **Design.** Details the system design, including the data model, algorithms, and interfaces.
- **Interfaces.** Defines the interfaces between the system and other systems or external components.
- **Security.** Details security requirements and design for the system, including access control mechanisms and data encryption methods.
- **Scaling.** Defines the system's approach to scaling, including load-balancing mechanisms and failover strategies.
- **Deployment.** The system's deployment strategy, including the hardware and software environment, and other infrastructure requirements. It will also include a deployment diagram that illustrates the physical deployment components and how they interact with each other and with external systems.
- **Conclusion.** Summarizes the main design decisions and their rationale.
- **References.** Lists the sources used in the document, including standards and best practices followed.
- **Appendices.** Other information that's useful but not essential to the document.

Your document's structure needs to be appropriate to what you're doing, and that structure can help you do it well. The sections help you corral the information in a way that's meaningful, easy to take in at a glance (that is, it's scannable), and easier to understand. Good structure adds clarity.

How do you know how to structure any given document?

Step one is to look inside your organization. There may be an existing template to use or a document you can model. Start there.

Using a structure that's already known within your organization helps meet reader expectations. They know what kind of information the document will contain, where, and why.

If there's no existing template you can use, step two is querying your favorite search engine. You'll find plenty of outlines and examples to follow. Look at a few, notice how they are the same and how they differ, and adopt what's best for your purpose.

∾

**Exercise: Document Structure**

Choose a document type or analyze an existing technical document, and make a list of the key components of the document's structure.

As an example, I've chosen a high-level system design. You can see the key components of this in the *Appendix: Exercise Answers*.

# 9

# ORGANIZING AND FORMATTING

Y ou can support your document structure by organizing it to ensure that readers find it easy to follow, and you can make your writing look professional by using clear and consistent formatting.

Your chief tools here are:

- headings
- numbered headings
- lists
- tables
- white space
- consistent formatting
- styles.

Let's look at each of these.

## Headings

Headings, along with subheadings, act like signposts in your document. They tell the reader where they are and what to expect.

Have a look at the built-in heading styles in your word processor (more on styles later in this chapter, if you're not clear on how to use them). Here's a screenshot of the default Heading styles in my version of Microsoft Word:[1]

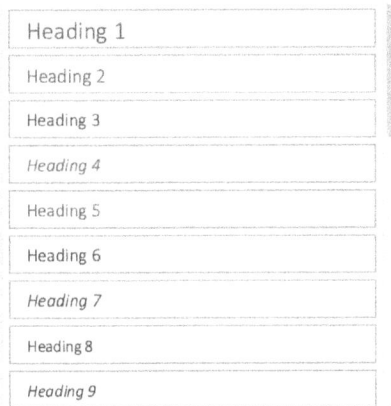

Word gives me nine different pre-defined heading and subheading styles to use. As you can see here, they each look different in some way, with the largest, most prominent one at the top, and the smallest, least prominent at the bottom.

If I use these headings consistently through my document, they give the reader a clear visual sense of the hierarchy of information. I strongly encourage you to use them.

Headings and subheadings are fantastic, but a word of warning: don't go too far down the rabbit hole. I don't like to go much further than two or three heading levels. Requiring more than that tends to suggest that there's a flaw in how the document is organized. So, even though Word offers me nine different heading levels, if I'm using Heading 5, I may have a problem.

~

## Numbered Headings

The Very Large Government Agency I worked for had a penchant for numbering their headings — so much so that their default template looked something like this:

Heading 1      ¶ª

Heading 2      ¶ª

Heading 3      ¶ª

Heading 4      ¶ª

Heading 5      ¶ª

Heading 1 (numbered)      ¶

Heading 2 (numbered)      ¶

Heading 3 (numbered)      ¶

Heading 4 (numbered)      ¶

Heading 5 (numbered)      ¶

Applied, these numbered headings look like something you might see in a legal document, or in some cases (especially at the Very Large Government Agency), a technical document:

## 1.     Heading 1 (numbered)

Text goes here.

### 1.1.     Heading 2 (numbered)

This is our first subheader.

#### 1.1.1.     Heading 3 (numbered)

And a sub-subheader.

##### 1.1.1.1.     Heading 4 (numbered)

Yet another nested subheader.

###### 1.1.1.1.1.     Heading 5 (numbered)

Five levels of nesting really is too much.

In many contexts, this kind of numbering is very useful, especially if your readers will need to reference specific sections in the document. The high-level system designs and system security architectures I was involved with used numbered headings because they were long, technical, detailed documents, and it was easy to get lost.

But I don't default to this style of heading, as I feel the numbers too often get in the way. If I can reasonably avoid them, I will.

~

### Lists

There are two kinds of lists: ordered (numbered) lists and unordered (dot point) lists. I go into these in greater detail in the next chapter, *Bullets and Numbers*.

For now, know that lists are great for presenting information clearly and concisely by breaking it into smaller, easier-to-understand chunks. They let you take a sentence like this:

> *To improve its productivity, the team agreed to conduct daily stand-ups, institute a weekly reporting process on Confluence, hold quarterly one-on-ones with the section head, and twice a month, there will be a 30-minute information social gathering.*

And turn it into this:

*To improve productivity, the team agreed to:*

- *daily stand-ups*
- *weekly reporting on Confluence*
- *quarterly one-on-ones with the section head*
- *twice monthly 30-minute informal social gatherings.*

That's much more easily read.

∼

## Tables

Like lists, tables are a fantastic organizational tool. They can convey information quickly, while making it easier to compare or relate different things. If you're facing a big block of text, ask yourself, "Would this work as a table?"

For example:

> *Each fault found must be classified according to how likely it is to happen, considering the chance of it happening (the qualitative assessment of likelihood), the frequency of it happening (how often it happens), and the probability (a statistical amount of likelihood). Chance can be one of the following: has occurred in the last year; has occurred more than once in the past; has occurred at least once; has not occurred within the organization, but has at other departments; or, is possible, but does not have known occurrences. Frequency can be: ten or more times in the past decade, or known circumstances mean it will almost certainly happen; has occurred seven times in the past decade, or known circumstances mean it will likely happen in the next few years; has occurred three times in the past decade, and circumstances mean it is reasonably likely in the next few years; has occurred two or three times in the past decade in other, similar organizations; has occurred only a few times in the past 50 years. Probability should be assessed as greater than 95%, greater than 60%, greater than 30%, less than 30%, or less than 5%.*

Did you manage to get through that? I bet you stopped reading about 25 words in.

Adding white space (more on that below) can help. In the example below, all I've done is broken that same piece of text into several paragraphs.

*Each fault found must be classified according to how likely it is to happen, considering the chance of it happening (the qualitative assessment of likelihood), the frequency of it happening (how often it happens), and the probability (a statistical amount of likelihood).*

*Chance can be one of the following: has occurred in the last year; has occurred more than once in the past; has occurred at least once; has not occurred within the organization, but has at other departments; or, is possible, but does not have known occurrences.*

*Frequency can be: ten or more times in the past decade, or known circumstances mean it will almost certainly happen; has occurred seven times in the past decade, or known circumstances mean it will likely happen in the next few years; has occurred three times in the past decade, and circumstances mean it is reasonably likely in the next few years; has occurred two or three times in the past decade in other, similar organizations; has occurred only a few times in the past 50 years.*

*Probability should be assessed as greater than 95%, greater than 60%, greater than 30%, less than 30%, or less than 5%.*

That helped, some. But a table makes this a lot easier. Have a look at the table in the image below.

| Risk Likelihood Scale | | |
|---|---|---|
| **Chance**<br><br>*The qualitative assessment of likelihood* | **Frequency**<br><br>*How often it happens* | **Probability**<br><br>*The statistical likelihood* |
| Has occurred in the last year | >10 times in the past decade, or known circumstances mean it will **almost certainly** happen | >95% |
| Has occurred more than once in the past | 7 or more occurrences times in the past decade, or known circumstances mean it will **likely** happen in the next few years | >60% |
| Has occurred at least once | 3 or more times in the past decade, and circumstances mean it is **reasonably likely** in the next few years | >30% |
| Has not occurred within the organization, but has at other departments | 2 or 3 times in the past decade in other, similar organizations | <30% |
| Is possible, but no known occurrences | Has occurred a few times in the past 50 years | <5% |

Much easier to understand, no?

Note that I don't usually use bold for emphasis, the way I have here in the Frequency column. I prefer to emphasize using *italics*. But I've used bold here because I want those particular words to pop out at the reader, making this table more glanceable.

∿

## White Space

White space is the empty space on the page, and is a key factor in making your text readable. When your readers face a wall of uninterrupted text, something switches off in their brains and comprehension is reduced.

Glance back through this chapter, and consider how I've used white space. The lists, the images, the table, the headings, the subheadings, the indented examples — all of these things help break up the text. This makes it easier on the eye and avoids cramming too much information onto a page. So, too, do the choice of margins, line spacing, and paragraph spacing.

White space makes your document more user-friendly. Use it liberally.

~

## Consistent Formatting

One thing *not* to be liberal about is your formatting. Your documents should stick to a few, consistent, simple formatting options. This includes fonts, font sizes, margins, and indentation and spacing.

### FONTS

If your document looks like a ransom note made of letters cut from a dozen magazines, you're doing it wrong. Most documents are fine with one font — or maybe two, if you want one for headings and another for the main body text. But more than two, and things start looking junky. Keep it simple.

Your choice of font depends on a lot of factors. Your organization might have preferred fonts in their branding guidelines. If so, use those. If not, for technical documents, stick with boring. You don't want your chosen font to call attention to itself. (I'm looking at you,

Comic Sans.) Helvetica is nice, solid, venerable font. Or you could use its poor cousin, Arial. I'm fond of Garamond as well.

But whatever you do, stick with one or two for the whole document.

### Font Sizes

Consistent font sizes help your reader focus on what they're reading. If you've ever seen a document that jumps from an eleven-point font up to a twelve, and then down to a ten, you'll know they're hard to read. For the main body of your document, pick a size (I like an eleven-point font) and stick with it.

### Margins

Allow yourself a roomy margin — again, this helps readability. I typically use 2.5 centimeters (an inch) on all sides. Again, keep your margins uniform throughout the document.

### Indentation and Spacing

Consistent line spacing, paragraph spacing, and indentation help keep the document readable.

Again, look at the way I've formatted this chapter. Where have I used indents? (The example texts.) Have I changed the line spacing or the paragraph spacing? (No.) As I said before, make a choice, and stick with it.

~

### Using Styles in a Word Processor

Styles are predefined sets of formatting characteristics that typically apply to paragraphs (although some styles apply only to the characters, rather than the entire paragraph). Most full-feature word processors support using styles. Some are built in as defaults, but you can also create custom styles to format text using your particular choices.

I use styles, literally, daily. I encourage you to do the same, as they help ensure your formatting is consistent, and you can change them all at the click of a button.

The screen capture below is taken from Word, and shows how a custom Heading 1 style might be defined:

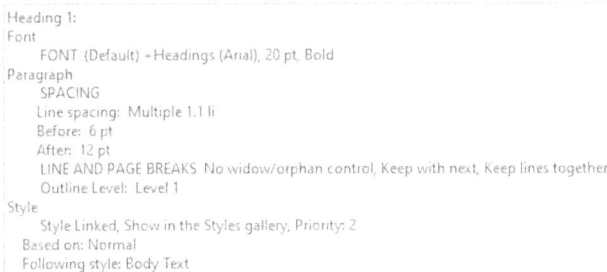

```
Heading 1:
Font
        FONT (Default) +Headings (Arial), 20 pt, Bold
Paragraph
        SPACING
        Line spacing: Multiple 1.1 li
        Before: 6 pt
        After: 12 pt
        LINE AND PAGE BREAKS No widow/orphan control, Keep with next, Keep lines together
        Outline Level: Level 1
Style
        Style Linked, Show in the Styles gallery, Priority: 2
    Based on: Normal
    Following style: Body Text
```

Without getting into all the detail, you can see, broadly, that a paragraph assigned this Heading 1 style will have these characteristics:

- The text will appear in 20-point Arial font in bold.
- The line spacing will be 1.1 lines. (Line spacing doesn't matter too much here, since this is for headings, which are typically on one line only.)
- The paragraph will have six points of space before it and 12 points of space after it.
- The paragraph will be kept with the one that follows, and the lines won't split across a page. This is important, as you don't want your heading orphaned at the bottom of a page. You want it glued to the text that follows.
- When you press enter at the end of the line, the subsequent paragraph will have the style Body Text.

Learning to use styles is like gaining a superpower. Styles help you maintain the consistency we've been discussing — they ensure that all text with that particular style will look the same.

They also allow you to make changes quickly and efficiently. Let's say you decide you want all your major headings to be 22 points, not 20 points. If you've applied styles, then all you have to do is change the style definition, and the change will automatically be made throughout your document. Amazing.

Styles are easy to apply, too. You just select the text, click the style name, and boom. Done.

If you need more instruction on how to use styles, your friendly neighborhood search engine can help. Just type in "How to use styles in Word." Better yet, find a video on YouTube. There are a bazillion.

I hope I've convinced you to use styles. They're incredibly powerful. Familiarize yourself with them, and make them part of your writing routine.

~

**Exercise: Organizing Information**

Here are some exercises to help with organizing your information. See the *Appendix: Exercise Answers* for my versions.

1. Rewrite the following sentence using dot points to make it more readable.

> The application, built on a microservices architecture, utilizes a combination of RESTful APIs for synchronous communication, message queues for asynchronous communication, and a service mesh to provide a uniform way to connect, secure, and manage traffic between services, ultimately enhancing the system's scalability, fault tolerance, and maintainability.

2. Rewrite the following sentence by adding white space to make it more readable.

In recent years, containerization technology has gained significant traction in the software development industry, particularly in the context of deploying and managing microservices-based applications. Containerization allows developers to package applications, along with their dependencies, into lightweight, portable, and self-sufficient units known as containers. These containers can then be deployed across various environments with minimal modification, simplifying the development, testing, and deployment processes. Docker is one of the most popular containerization platforms, providing developers with a comprehensive set of tools and a rich ecosystem for managing containers. In conjunction with container orchestration platforms like Kubernetes, developers can efficiently manage container deployment, scaling, and networking. The combination of containerization and orchestration platforms promotes a more streamlined development process, enabling teams to rapidly deliver high-quality software while adhering to best practices for reliability, scalability, and maintainability.

# 10

# BULLETS AND NUMBERED LISTS

L et's say you've decided to enter the holiday season cubicle-decorating contest. Your co-worker, Sandii, always wins, but this year, you're determined to take home the prize. The competition is fierce, though. Winning this thing is going to take some serious organization.

You open your note-taking app ready to type out your plans, and realize there's a critical decision you have to make.

Do you make your Cubicle Decorating Glory To-Do list with bullet points, or do you use a numbered list?

Bullets vs. numbers. Gah!

Suddenly, you're paralyzed. It's almost enough to let Sandii keep on winning.

Hey. Don't worry.

You got this. You just need to know a simple rule:

*If the order matters, use numbers.*

*If the order does not matter, use bullet points.*

We have our rule, so let's figure this out. Start with the items that need to go on the list, but ignore bullets and numbers:

Decorate the office according to your plan, deploying the forklift as needed.

Borrow a forklift to help with the heavy lifting.

Buy lights, streamers, tinsel, canned snow, and other accoutrements.

Find out when the judges are coming.

Decide on a theme for your cubicle decorations.

Explain to the judges the history and motivation behind the chosen theme.

Create a shopping list of items to buy.

Research and incorporate sustainable decorating options to reduce environmental impact, and to incorporate all known relevant holidays (Christmas, Chanukah, Kwanzaa, Festivus, etc.).

Deliver the acceptance speech.

Prepare an acceptance speech.

Run quality assurance tests on all the lights and decorations to make sure they work properly.

Hire a marching band to play during the judges' visit.

Use CAD software to plan the decoration layout.

Humbly accept the blue ribbon from the judges.

Lead the marching band through the office just as the judges arrive.

That'll do for now.

Clearly, some of this has to happen in a certain order. You can't lead the marching band before you hire them. But you can prepare your acceptance speech before or after you borrow the forklift.

Let's try putting things in a better sequence. And since we're talking about a sequence, let's make it an ordered list and use numbers:

1. Decide on a theme for your cubicle decorations.
2. Research and incorporate sustainable decorating options to reduce environmental impact, and to incorporate all known relevant holidays (Christmas, Chanukah, Kwanzaa, Festivus, etc.).
3. Create a shopping list of items to buy.
4. Buy lights, streamers, tinsel, canned snow, and other accoutrements.
5. Borrow a forklift to help with the heavy lifting.
6. Hire a marching band to play during the judges' visit.
7. Prepare an acceptance speech.
8. Find out when the judges are coming.
9. Use CAD software to plan the decoration layout.
10. Run quality assurance tests on all the lights and decorations to make sure they work properly.
11. Decorate the office according to your plan, deploying the forklift as needed.
12. Lead the marching band through the office just as the judges arrive.
13. Explain to the judges the history and motivation behind the chosen theme.
14. Humbly accept the blue ribbon from the judges.
15. Deliver the acceptance speech.

Like I said, that sort of works, but it does mix things that could be done in any order with things that can't.

Let's break the list in two, so there's a Preparation Phase and an Execution Phase.

**Preparation Phase**

- Decide on a theme for your cubicle decorations.
- Research and incorporate sustainable decorating options to reduce environmental impact, and to incorporate all known relevant holidays (Christmas, Chanukah, Kwanzaa, Festivus, etc.).
- Create a shopping list of items to buy.
- Buy lights, streamers, tinsel, canned snow, and other accoutrements.
- Find out when the judges are coming.
- Borrow a forklift to help with the heavy lifting.
- Hire a marching band to play during the judges' visit.
- Prepare an acceptance speech.

**Execution Phase**

1. Use CAD software to plan the decoration layout.
2. Run quality assurance tests on all the lights and decorations to make sure they work properly.
3. Decorate the office according to your plan, deploying the forklift as needed.
4. Lead the marching band through the office just as the judges arrive.
5. Explain to the judges the history and motivation behind the chosen theme.
6. Humbly accept the blue ribbon from the judges.
7. Deliver the acceptance speech.

The tasks in the Preparation Phase don't need to be done in a particular order. (Okay, you could argue that you need to decide on a theme before you create a shopping list. And you probably need to know when the judges are coming so you can tell the band when you need it to be there. Let's set those aside for the moment.) In general, the order of these things doesn't matter, so we use bullet points.

The steps in the Execution Phase need to be done in sequence, however, so we present these as an ordered list with numbers.

How does this look in your technical documents? Pretty much the same.

Sometimes in tech documents, the order of things doesn't matter. A list of infrastructure items or the tools a team uses can go in any order, although you might put the most important ones toward the top. However, if you're writing a standard operating procedure or the instructions for accomplishing a particular task, the steps need to be presented in sequence, and numbers are your friend.

An example of an unordered list:

*For test automation, the team uses the following tools:*

- *UFT*
- *LeanFT*
- *Selenium*
- *Java*
- *Rest Assured*
- *Maven*
- *SoapUI.*

An example of an ordered list:

*To get access to the server, make a request through the Company Request System (CRS), as follows:*

1. *Go to the intranet home page and click the Company Request System button. This takes you to the Company Request System main screen.*
2. *In the Search box, type "server access" and press Enter. CRS displays matching results.*
3. *Choose Grant Server Access and press Enter.*

4. *Click Request Access. This displays the Request Server Access screen.*
5. *Light a red candle.*
6. *Chant, "Oh, Great Network Administrator, I humbly request and beseech you to grant me sysadmin access to server abcooo.largecorp.net."*
7. *Repeat chant 19 times.*
8. *Check email for a response.*

See the difference?

By the way, note the punctuation I've used in the above two examples. For the bulleted list, I didn't put any punctuation at the end of each line. I've just used a single period at the end of the final one. That's because the items listed are short — a word or two — and a period would look odd after each.

In the numbered list, however, I've put a period at the end of each one, as they are full sentences.

As I rule, I don't use semicolons (";") or simple commas at the end of list items. I use full stops, question marks (where appropriate), or nothing.

～

PRO TIP #1: IF YOUR LIST ONLY HAS ONE ITEM, DON'T USE A BULLET format. It looks silly. So don't do this:

*This is a short list:*

- *Really it is.*

Rewrite the text so it doesn't have the bullet.

*This really is a short list.*

Pro tip #2: If your sequence only has two steps, don't use a number format. Again, it looks silly. Example:

*Does your process only have two steps? If so:*

*Rewrite the sentences.*

*Don't use numbers like this.*

∿

### Exercise: Ordered vs. Unordered Lists (Numbers vs. Bullets)

Rewrite the following sample paragraphs as either an ordered (numbered) or unordered (bulleted) list. Each paragraph lends itself to one or the other. See the *Appendix: Exercise Answers* for my versions.

### Sample 1

When selecting a database management system for your project, there are several factors to consider. You should take into account the scalability requirements, data consistency needs, query complexity, ease of maintenance, and the overall performance of the system. By evaluating these factors, you can make a more informed decision about which database management system is best suited for your project.

### Sample 2

To set up a new virtual machine using VirtualBox, start by downloading and installing the latest version of VirtualBox on your host machine. Next, open VirtualBox and click on the "New" button to create a new virtual machine. Then, choose the operating system and allocate the required RAM and storage. Finally, boot the virtual machine and complete the operating system installation process.

## Sample 3

Let's configure a new web server using Nginx. First, install Nginx on your server. Next, create a new server block configuration file for your domain. Then, edit the configuration file to specify the root directory, server name, and location blocks. After that, test the configuration for syntax errors and reload Nginx to apply the changes. Lastly, verify that the web server is serving your website correctly by accessing it through a web browser.

## Sample 4

When evaluating different cloud service providers for your business, there are several key aspects to consider. Factors such as pricing, available services, global infrastructure, security features, and support options should all play a role in your decision-making process. By carefully assessing these aspects, you can select the most suitable cloud service provider for your specific needs.

## Sample 5

Implementing a successful Continuous Integration (CI) and Continuous Deployment (CD) pipeline requires integrating several tools and practices. You will need to set up version control, automate the build process, perform automated testing, handle deployment, and monitor your application's performance. By incorporating these elements, you can streamline your development process and improve the overall quality of your software.

## Sample 6

To create a new Python virtual environment, ensure you have Python and pip installed on your system. Next, install the "virtualenv" package using pip. Create a new directory for your project and navigate to it in the terminal. After that, run the "virtualenv" command to create a new virtual environment within the directory. Activate the virtual environment to start using it for your project.

## 11

SEND YOUR COMMAS TO OXFORD

In some circles, this chapter is controversial.

I suggest you ignore the hoo-hah, and just take my advice. What advice is that?

*Embrace Oxford commas. Use them all the time.*

An Oxford comma, also called a serial comma, is the comma you put before "and" or "or" when you have a sentence that lists three or more things. So, "apple, orange and banana" does not have an Oxford comma. "Apple, orange, and banana" does (the one after "orange").

I'm a big fan of Oxford commas, because I think they add clarity.

Others disagree. For example, the Very Large Government Agency that I once worked for had a writing style guide that specifically said you don't need them unless there's an ambiguity.

This is a reasonable position for them to take. But I still suggest you use them.

Author Lynne Truss, in her book *Eats, Shoots & Leaves: The Zero Tolerance Approach to Punctuation*, wrote, "There are people who embrace the Oxford comma, and people who don't, and I'll just say this: never get between these people when drink has been taken."[1]

Solid advice, that.

"What's the big deal?" I hear you ask. "It's just a comma. Who cares?"

George Washington and Abraham Lincoln. They care.

Consider this example.

> *We visited the orangutans, Washington, and Lincoln.*
>
> *We visited the orangutans, Washington and Lincoln.*

What's the difference between those two sentences? In the first one, with the serial comma, it's clear that we visited orangutans, as well as Washington and Lincoln. In the second one, it sounds like we visited orangutans who were named Washington and Lincoln.

That comma makes a big difference to how we understand the sentence.

Let me make another plea for the Oxford comma: it can save you money.

In 2014, three truckers sued a company called Oakhurst Dairy, seeking four years' worth of overtime. Under Maine statute, drivers were entitled to time-and-a-half if they worked more than 40 hours in a week. But the law gave exemptions in the following situations:

> *The canning, processing, preserving, freezing, drying, marketing, storing, packing for shipment or distribution of:*
>
> *(1) Agricultural produce;*
>
> *(2) Meat and fish products; and*

(3) *Perishable foods.*

Because there was no comma after "packing for shipment," the law's meaning was ambiguous. Was it supposed to mean that the "packing for shipment" and "distribution" of the three listed categories were exempt? Or did it mean that "packing for shipment or distribution" was exempt, but not the distribution itself?

If "shipment" had had a comma after it, it would have been clear. Distribution would have been exempt. But it wasn't there, so it went to court.

Oakhurst Dairy settled the dispute for $5 million.[2]

That's a lot of money for a comma.

So, yes. I'm a fan of the Oxford, and I encourage you to be one as well.

But, whether you adopt the serial comma or reject them except where they're absolutely needed, you need to be consistent. Make sure you use them (or not) in the same way all through your document. That will be less confusing to your readers.

∼

## Exercise: Oxford Commas

Consider the following sentences, and note how the Oxford comma changes the meaning of each. See the *Appendix: Exercise Answers* for explanations.

### Example 1

a. The conference attendees included the team managers, Alice and Bob.

b. The conference attendees included the team managers, Alice, and Bob.

**Example 2**

a. The bug was discovered by the quality assurance specialist, a hacker and a programmer.

b. The bug was discovered by the quality assurance specialist, a hacker, and a programmer.

**Example 3**

a. The software was developed by the lead engineer, a perfectionist and a workaholic.

b. The software was developed by the lead engineer, a perfectionist, and a workaholic.

# 12

## ACRONYMS

W hat does "DWATRW" stand for?

Right there, you can see the problem with acronyms (abbreviations formed using the first letter of other words). You can never[1] assume your reader knows what an acronym means, and the same one can mean different things in different contexts.

DWATRW stands for Dealing With Acronyms The Right Way.

Because there's a right way and a wrong way.

The right way is to spell out an acronym the first time you use it in a document. If the document you're writing has a glossary, you can put it in there as well, although you can't assume your reader will actually *look* at the glossary. (I mean, when was the last time *you* looked at one?) So spell the acronym out on first use, then put it in parentheses immediately after.

Example:

*This agreement between the Department of Large Government Stuff (DLGS) and the Extremely Small and Not Very Powerful Corporation, Incorporated (ESNVPC) covers all uses of the Three-Letter Acronym Generating Software (TLAGen).*

The more formal the document, the more you need to do this.

When I said you can never assume your reader knows what an acronym stands for, I meant it. Never.

Okay, that's "never" in the Gilbert and Sullivan's *HMS Pinafore* sense. You know the scene:

*Captain: "... And I'm never, never sick at sea."*

*Chorus: "What, never?"*

*Captain: "No, never!"*

*Chorus: "What, never?"*

*Captain: "Hardly ever!"*

*Not* spelling out acronyms is a "hardly ever" kind of thing, but there are some I'd use without hesitation in technical documents (depending, as always, on the audience and document purpose). I wouldn't put "International Business Machines (IBM)" if I was writing about that company in a strategy document, for example. In most contexts, I figure that people know what IBM refers to. The same goes for NASA, scuba, CPU, DNA, JPEG, LAN, LCD, LED, VHS, UV... You get the idea. There are a certain number of abbreviations (a.m., p.m., etc., no., B.C., A.D.) and acronyms that it's safe to assume your reader will know. (I spoke about assumed knowledge in the *Adapting to Audiences* chapter.)

This assumption about acronyms also exists locally within organizations.

If I was writing something for internal use at the Department of Large Government Stuff, and everybody commonly referred to it by its acronym, DLGS, then I probably wouldn't spell it out on first use. The less formal the communication (emails, for example), the less the need to spell it all out. But if I was writing a high-level policy or strategy document, I'd still spell it out the first time, and put it in the glossary, just to make sure.

There might even be a style guide within your agency that dictates the correct form of an acronym, stating that for the Department of Large Government Stuff, it is "DLGS" and not "DoLGS" or just "LGS." (I talk about style guides in the *Style Guides* chapter.)

One more thing.

It is the nature of organizations and agencies (especially government ones) to have their names change. The DLGS may once have been the Department of Large Items (DLI), and before that, the Big Things Agency (BTA).

I was at the Very Large Government Agency when they went through a name change, and the most obvious acronym for the new name was already taken by another, not-so-large agency. Management made a point of saying not to use the obvious acronym, so the two would not be confused. They formalized this preference in their style guide.[2]

If you're writing a document that's going to stick around for a while (like policies and strategies), spelling out acronyms helps future-proof the document. This means that readers in the future, who might not know what the situation was when the document was created, have a better chance of understanding what you've written.

**Exercise: Acronyms**

Pick a document that you've recently written or that you've come across in your work, and consider its acronyms.

1. Make a list of the acronyms in the document.
2. Write out the meaning for each.
3. Considering the audience, decide if each term can be assumed knowledge or not.
4. Considering your audience, decide if each term should be in a glossary for the document or not.
5. Rewrite one or two paragraphs that include acronyms to properly introduce them.

I've done this for a sample paragraph in the *Appendix: Exercise Answers* to give you a feel for it.

# 13

## NUMBERS

### Basic Rules

Technical documents use a lot of numbers. Whether you're talking about measurements, prices, hardware capacities, uptime percentages, sizes, or speeds, numbers are everywhere.

You need to be mindful of how you write numbers. You want to make sure that they contribute to readability and aren't distracting. The most suitable approach will depend on the type of document you're writing, and the prevalence of numbers (especially large ones) within it.

When typing numbers into a document, these are the basic rules I follow:

- Spell out integers up to and including eleven.[1]
- Use numerals for integers from 12 and up.
- Always use numerals for decimal numbers.

- Don't start a sentence with a numeral. Either write the number in words, or rewrite the sentence so the number appears later.

(Note: these are my rules for technical documents. I have different rules for non-technical writing, like my fiction.)

Some examples are below.

≈

**Don't ⇒ Do**

*The report was 5 pages long.* ⇒ The report was five pages long.
*The test took forty-three seconds.* ⇒ The test took 43 seconds.
*Pi is approximately three point one four one five nine two six five three.* ⇒ Pi is approximately 3.141592653.
*200 people attended the conference.* ⇒ Two hundred people attended the conference.

≈

OTHERS DISAGREE WITH SOME ASPECTS OF MY APPROACH.

*The Australian Government Style Manual*, for example, advises that you use numerals for "2" and up, and should write the numbers "zero" and "one" using words.

When I read that, I thought, "No way I'm adopting that. I totally disagree." (But maybe don't tell the Very Large Government Agency that.)

*The Publication Manual of the American Psychological Association* (APA), another widely used style guide, tells us, with exceptions, to use words for numbers from zero through nine, and numerals for 10 and above. This is pretty common advice, and is reasonable.

*The Chicago Manual of Style* says to use words from zero through one hundred, and numerals for 101 and up. Again, this is reasonable advice, but is probably better suited to non-technical documents.

With all these differing opinions, who's right?

I am, of course. Use my rules, unless they contradict the style guide your organization uses, or if a different approach suits you better.

But whatever you do, be consistent.

∾

**Bonus Rules**

In addition to the rules above, there are a few more guidelines that can help you figure out specific situations.

- Use numbers when you are talking about measurements. Example: The container held 20 liters of radioactive water, and was found 8 kilometers from the waste disposal site.
- Use numbers for percentages. Example: The test used 88% of CPU capacity.
- Use words for common fractions, and numbers for all other fractions. Example: I ate two-thirds of my donut. The box has 1/6 of them left.
- Use words if the number appears in the title of a document. Example: "A Summary of Twelve Key Findings from the Review Committee."
- Use numbers in dates. Example: "She was born on March 9, 1955."
- Use commas if your number has four or more digits. Example: "Testers filed 2,500 bug reports."
- Use numbers and words together if you have a large number that's being rounded. Example: "Our budget exceeded $20 billion last year."

~

**Exercise: Numbers**

Rewrite the following sentences to correct the way the numbers are given. My versions are in the *Appendix: Exercise Answers*.

1. The three-D printer finished 7 models in 4 hours, and 5 more were left.
2. 6 developers completed ninety percent of the project, while the remaining ten% was done by a 7th developer.
3. 30 servers handle 70% of the load, and the other 30% is distributed among 10 additional servers.
4. The ten terabyte hard drive has a seven thousand, two hundred RPM speed and two hundred fifty six MB of cache.
5. On 8th of September 2022, the software release included 6 major updates and 20 bug fixes.
6. The team has 5 data scientists, 3 software engineers, and 2 project managers.
7. 70% of users prefer the mobile app, while 30% use the desktop version.
8. There are 4 main operations supported by the API: create, read, update, and delete.
9. 5% of the devices failed the quality assurance test due to 2 critical issues.
10. 3 main goals of the project are increasing performance, reducing costs by fifty percent, and improving user experience.

# 14

## UNNECESSARY CAPITALIZATION

Have a look at this paragraph:

*The Vendor will be responsible for the delivery of the new Customer System. The Customer System will support a User Experience that allows the Users to connect with Service Staff through a dedicated, custom-made Chat Client.*

Anything strike you as strange? (Hint: consider the nouns.)

Let me run that through Google Translate:

*Der Verkäufer ist für die Lieferung des neuen Kundensystems verant-wortlich. Das Kundensystem unterstützt eine Benutzererfahrung, die es den Benutzern ermöglicht, sich über einen dedizierten, maßgeschneiderten Chat-Client mit dem Servicepersonal zu verbinden.*

Ah, that's better.

"Verkäufer," "Lieferung," "Kundensystem," "Benutzererfahrung," "Benutzer," "Chat-Client," "Verbindung," and "Servicepersonal" are all plain, old regular nouns. In German, the first letter in a noun is always capitalized, which is why the paragraph above looks as it does.

In English, we only capitalize proper nouns (like names and titles), not regular nouns. So, we'd write, "Get your behind off my Cadillac and haul on over to the store." The nouns are "behind" and "store," and they're all regular lower-case words. "Cadillac," being the name of the car, is a proper noun, so it gets capitalized.

I think in technical documents, people sometimes capitalize words like "vendor," "user experience," and "service staff" (as I have in the example above) because those terms are important to what they're trying to say. Capitalizing those words gives them an emphasis that lower case seems to lack.

Don't do that.

Here's our first paragraph again, appropriately capitalized.

> *The vendor will be responsible for the delivery of the new customer system. The customer system will support a user experience that allows the users to connect with service staff through a dedicated chat client.*

Leave things that aren't proper nouns lower case. It'll be easier to read.

While we're here, take a moment to see if you can simplify those two sentences to improve readability.

Here's my crack at it:

> *The vendor is responsible for delivering the new customer system, which supports users connecting with service staff through a dedicated, custom chat client.*

Do you see how this is more direct, has fewer and simpler words, less repetition, but still conveys the same idea? That's what we're going for.

Of course, if New Customer System was the actual name of the system, like Microsoft Word or Confluence or Jira, then you'd capitalize it. Similarly, if Service Staff was the actual name of the team providing the service, like Customer Relations or Customer Success Heroes (please, don't do that to your organization), you'd capitalize that, too. But not if they're just generic words.

~

### Exercise: Unnecessary Capitalization

Rewrite the following paragraphs and correct the capitalization mistakes. See the *Appendix: Exercise Answers* for my take.

### Example 1

The software Development team used python for their new Web Application. They chose Flask as the Web Framework, and the Database management system was postgresql. the team used Git for Version Control and they hosted the repository on Github. they used the Agile Methodology, including scrum for project Management.

### Example 2

the Network engineers were tasked with setting up a virtual Private Network (VPN) for Remote Employees. They selected the Openvpn protocol and configured the Firewall to allow connections on Port 1194. They also provided Step-By-Step Instructions to help employees install and configure the vpn Client software on their devices.

### Example 3

Machine Learning algorithms, such as Decision Trees, K-Nearest Neighbors, and Support Vector Machines, were evaluated for the Data Analysis project. The Team used Python Libraries, like Scikit-Learn, Pandas, and Numpy, to process the Data and train the models. The Model with the best Accuracy was chosen for implementation in the Production environment.

# 15

## JARGON

Let's start by defining what jargon is. Jargon is specialized language that is particular to a specific profession or field. Take this sentence, for example:

*We're using Agile all through the SDLC, to ensure we meet our KPIs and hit our release on time.*

Do you understand that? Would your boss? Your grandmother?

"Agile," "SDLC," "KPIs," and "release" (in this context) are all terms specific to software development and management, and are examples of jargon. Understanding the sentence above requires you know something about that domain. If you don't, then what I've written is, I'm sure, both confusing and off-putting.

Let me remove the jargon:

*We're using the Agile development methodology through all stages of the software development process to ensure we meet our goals and deliver on time.*

The problem is, one person's jargon is another person's efficient communication. The second version is understandable to a wider readership, but uses more words and is less precise.

Here's another example:

> *The repair required us to replace the corroded gal with PVC and connect them using a wye fitting, then seal the joints with Teflon and install a vent to ensure proper DWV.*

You might understand that if you know about plumbing. But in case you don't, here it is without the jargon:

> *The repair involved replacing the rusted steel pipes with plastic ones, and connecting them with a Y-shaped pipe fitting. The joints were then sealed with a Teflon tape, then a pipe was added to allow air to flow in and out of the system.*

The second one is much more accessible, but isn't how you'd talk plumber-to-plumber.

Even within specific fields, there's jargon that might be impenetrable. If you're a computer person, consider this list of acronyms:

- CICS
- COBOL
- DASD
- IMS
- JCL
- MVS
- RACF
- VTAM.

Those come from mainframe computing. Here, let me spell them out:

- CICS — Customer Information Control System
- COBOL — COmmon Business Oriented Language
- DASD — Direct Access Storage Device
- IMS — Information Management System
- JCL — Job Control Language
- MVS — Multiple Virtual Storage
- RACF — Resource Access Control Facility
- VTAM — Virtual Telecommunications Access Method.

Even with the acronyms defined, these terms are still jargon and are unlikely to make sense to anyone who isn't an IBM mainframe person.

How does this apply to your writing?

In general, my advice is to avoid jargon where you can. It will make your writing clearer to more people.

How do you know if jargon is acceptable for a particular document?

You have to do what we discussed at the beginning of this book — define your audience. If you know for sure that they understand the subject, then technical terms and domain-specific language are fine.

But, on the whole, I try to avoid jargon. Here are some tips for doing just that (again, adapting them to the target audience):

- **Plain language.** Use plain language where you can. Using common words and phrases instead of technical ones makes your writing easier to grasp. Similarly, simple sentences are easier to follow than long, complex ones.
- **Definitions.** If you're using jargon that your audience won't necessarily be familiar with, define the term the first time you use it.
- **Glossary.** In technical or longer documents, consider including your jargon in a glossary.

- **Examples.** Use examples drawn from real-world situations to illustrate complex ideas. These make the ideas easier to understand.
- **Visuals.** Diagrams, graphs, tables, and illustrations can all help get your meaning across.
- **Reviewers.** Get another eye on your document. If you're not sure you're being clear, have someone in the target audience read it over.

~

**Exercise: Jargon**

Rewrite the following paragraphs to remove jargon or introduce it appropriately. See the *Appendix: Exercise Answers* for my take.

The application's back-end is implemented using a MEAN stack, which includes MongoDB, Express, Angular, and Node.js. The team decided to use this architecture due to its advantages in horizontal scalability and rapid development. Moreover, the application leverages RESTful APIs for the CRUD operations on the database.

The front-end of the application uses several advanced JavaScript frameworks, such as React, Redux, and GraphQL. These libraries enable the developers to create a highly responsive and maintainable user interface. Additionally, the front-end employs AJAX to asynchronously load data and update the UI without requiring a full page reload.

# 16

## SIMILES, METAPHORS, AND ANALOGIES

In the chapter *Adapting to Audiences*, I talked about analogies, and how they help explain something by comparing two different things to explain or clarify a complex idea by relating them. I gave this example:

> *A computer network is like a hotel with connected rooms, where each room is a computer, and each room number is an IP address.*

Let's dig into this form of expression.

There are three terms to know: similes, metaphors, and analogies. All three of these use the method of comparing things.

~

### Similes

For similes, think "similar". Similes indirectly compare two things that are similar, usually using "like" or "as" as the link between them.

Some examples:

- The data center is secure **like** a bank vault.
- Our server is as reliable **as** a rock.
- The code is as buggy **as** an ant farm.
- Her programming is **like** a Picasso.
- The business requirements are **as** clear as mud.
- The system ran **like** an aardvark wearing flip-flops.

Obviously, some of these are more suited to a technical document than others. But they demonstrate how using comparisons built with "as" and "like" can bring clarity to your meaning.

∼

## Metaphors

For metaphors, think "transfer" — as in, you are transferring one idea onto another to give a sense of the nature of something. Where similes indirectly compare, metaphors compare directly, using forms of the verb "to be," such as "is," "are," or "were."

Shakespeare knew a thing or two about metaphors. He used them all the time:

"But soft, what light through yonder window breaks?

It is the east, and Juliet is the sun!"

*Romeo & Juliet*

Here, he's transferring the idea of the sun onto Juliet to illustrate her radiance, as Romeo perceives it.

Or this one:

"All the world's a stage,

And all the men and women merely players;"

*As You Like It*

This time, he's transferring the idea life as a theatre drama onto the way people live out their day-to-day lives.

Some examples that are closer to home:

- Social media **is** the modern water cooler.
- Data **is** the oil of the new economy.
- Using the cloud for your servers **is** plugging into the mains grid instead of buying and running your own power generator.
- Software architecture **is** the blueprint, and software development **is** building the house.
- The internet **is** the information superhighway, and our intranet **is** the company's cul de sac.
- Highways **are** the arteries of domestic trade.

The right metaphor can bring clarity to your writing by helping readers understand complex ideas.

∾

## Analogies

Analogies typically do one or both of two things. They identify some kind of shared relationship, and/or they describe something unfamiliar using something familiar. They often have the logical structure of "A is to B," or "A is to B as C is to D."

Where similes are indirect comparisons and metaphors are direct comparisons, analogies can be called argumentative comparisons. They argue that two things that seem different are in a kind of relationship. They often use familiar information to teach about unfamiliar concepts.

Also, analogies can take the form of both similes and metaphors, so it can sometimes be hard to differentiate the three. The Venn diagram of similes, metaphors, and analogies has a lot of overlap.

But we're all in luck, because it doesn't really matter if an analogy is a simile or a metaphor or vice versa or whatever, because no one really cares. The point is to make the comparison, and thus bring understanding to your writing.

If the rock singer sings about life being a highway and wanting to ride all night long with you, that's an analogy (also a metaphor). They're establishing a relationship between life and the process of driving down a long road and spending that driving time in companionship with you, and they're doing so to clearly express their feelings about you.

If you say someone is like broken record, that's also an analogy (and a simile). The relationship we establish between that person and the malfunctioning piece of spinning vinyl presents their personality as one that goes over the same things repeatedly because they're stuck in a groove (which, by the way, is also an analogy).

When Forrest Gump talks about life being like a box of chocolates because you never know what you're going to get, that's also an analogy (and a simile).

Here are some examples that are more suited to the tech realm.

- A router is like the network's traffic cop.
- A bit is to computer science as an atom is to physics.
- The network's firewall is like the security guard for a building.
- You can think of processor speed as being like your car's horsepower.
- The Agile method's backlog is like a massive To-Do list.

If your technical document is explaining something to an audience that doesn't know what you're talking about, then using a good simile, metaphor, or analogy is like pulling the right tool out of the toolbox.

⁓

**Exercise: Similes and Metaphors**

Create a simile and a metaphor for the following technical concepts. You can see my take in the *Appendix: Exercise Answers.*

- Data encryption
- Network latency
- Cloud computing
- Load balancing
- Machine learning
- Distributed systems
- Cybersecurity
- Data compression

# 17

---

# PROOFREADING AND EDITING

P roofread your work.

It's that simple.

Before you click Send or Post or Publish or whatever, take the time to read over what you've written and ~~fox~~ fix the mistakes. They'll be there, so hunt them down and deal with them.

This applies to everything, from emails on up. The longer and more involved the document is, the more important it is to do this.

Here are some things that can help you in the proofreading and editing phase.

∾

## Take a Break

Taking a break between your writing phase and your editing phase can really help — especially for longer documents. The critical analysis and fault-finding that goes with your editing mind is different from the creativity and impulse to express that go with your writing mind. Whether a break means going to lunch for an hour or putting the piece away for a couple of days, that space gives you a chance to shift mental gears.

~

## Spelling (and Grammar) Check

I know this is the most obvious thing in the world, but it's such an easy step to skip: make sure you run a spelling check. If I had a nickel for every boo-boo, blunder, and flat-out bone-headed screw-up that a spelling check found over the years, I'd have a canyon's worth. It's so simple to do, it doesn't take long, and it helps you come across as more professional.

Also, while you're thinking about spelling, consider the language expectations of your audience. Do you need to use American English spelling? UK English? Australian English? Something else? If you're working for a government agency in England, the language expectations are different than if your intended audience is the CIO of an American tech firm.

For example, a few years ago, an Australian colleague of mine was signing off on an important tender document that had been prepared by an Aussie tech writer, but targeted to a major tech firm in the US. They received informal feedback that the document was considered sub-standard, even borderline illiterate, which surprised my colleague. Upon digging a little deeper she was told that it was the "poor spelling" and "obvious lack of proofreading" that had led her US counterpart to his conclusion. He had read UK spelling as typos and their prevalence as evidence of carelessness.

Obviously, not everyone will have that experience, but if you think your readers may trip over the language differences, it might be worth having two versions, one with American spelling and one with

UK spelling, or to at least pointing out the use of UK spelling at the top of the document.

~

## Out Loud

Here's a trick: read what you've written out loud. There's something about speaking the words aloud that engages a different part of your brain. Not only will this help you find mistakes, it also means you can hear when you've phrased something awkwardly, allowing you to make the changes you need.

Here's another variation of the trick: get Siri or Google Assistant or the built-in tech on your computer to read it out to you. This way, you can follow along and hear the mistakes as they're spoken. I use this all the time. Before I send a book to my editor, I always have Siri read the whole thing to me. My goal is to catch all of what I call "the stupids" (the missing words, incorrect tenses, mismatched subject-verb combinations — that kind of thing) to make her life easier by giving her less dumb stuff to fix.

~

## New Eyes

When you've gone over your writing several times, you stop being able to see your own words. Your brain starts filling in the pieces that ought to be there but aren't, and you stop finding the mistakes.

When this happens to me, I'll literally say, "I can't see this anymore."

That's when you bring in a second pair of eyes. Have someone else read what you've written. Because they're looking at it fresh, they're bound to find any problems that snuck past you.

Also, be discerning in who you ask. You need to have confidence that their changes will improve what you've written, not make it worse. Also, ask them to use tracked changes in their edits. That way you can decide whether you agree with their suggestions.

∼

### Exercise: Proofreading and Editing

Proofread and edit the following paragraphs, making any changes needed to fix errors and improve expression. My version is in the *Appendix: Exercise Answers*.

The companys new app has a Modular Fesign, which makes it easier to maintain and scale up. This is particularly important because the app is expected to grow rapidly in the coming months. In the past, the team faced several issues due to an tightly-coupled architecture and they wanted to avoid repeating the same mistakes again.

One of the key features of the app is its Integration with various 3$^{rd}$ Party Tools. Such integrations include 2-factor authentication, geolocation services, and Cloud-based Storage. Integrating these services can be complex, but the team has extensive experience with similar projects and have developed a set of best practices for streamlining the integration process.

# 18

---

# USER-TESTING YOUR DOCUMENT

Taking your document out for a spin is an excellent idea. This is particularly true if it:

- is meant to explain something, like a user guide or standard operating procedure
- will have a wide distribution, like a company-wide policy or strategy document
- will be used for a long time, like a five-year plan.

The more important and long-lived the document, the more I recommend doing some user acceptance testing (UAT).

This should be easy to do. Choose a volunteer from your target audience — or two, or six, depending on how wide the audience is — and have them read it. Then ask them questions to gauge their understanding.

If you're describing a business process or an operating procedure, have them follow your instructions, and see if they achieve the correct outcome.

If you've written something like a software manual or a quick start guide, then you can actually build documentation testing into your formal UAT process.

User-testing your document will demonstrate whether what you've written is clear, and the feedback you get should help you refine it.

∿

**Exercise: User-Test a Document**

Choose one of your documents, and have someone in your target audience read it and give you feedback. You can ask them to tell you about:

- anything that isn't clear
- whether the document tells them what they need to know
- anything they think could be said differently
- whether they found the document too easy, too hard, or about right
- any grammar or spelling mistakes
- if they stopped paying attention at any point, and if so, where
- any other suggested improvements.

## 19

DON'T. JUST DON'T

Some things I suggest you never do:[1]

- Don't put "xoxo" at the bottom of your work emails.
- Don't use emojis in technical and business documents. (However, they're more acceptable in informal communication.)
- Don't include lots of exclamation marks in your documents! I avoid them as much as I can! Sometimes, they may be appropriate in informal communication, like an email! But most documents are better without them! And if you feel you can justify an exclamation mark, don't use more than one!!!
- Don't use swear words. (Remember, different audiences have different ideas about what counts as a swear word, so be careful. I once had someone delete one of my posts in a Facebook group for using the term "w****r,"[2] and I thought, "Come on. I'm in Australia. That's practically a term of endearment." But ultimately, I decided they were right, because I'd crossed a community expectation about language use. My mistake.)

- Don't use sexist, racist, and other discriminatory and exclusionary language.
- Don't include jokes in a tech document.
- Don't include sexual or other inappropriate references in a document.
- Don't include a Dilbert cartoon in your PowerPoint.
- Don't plagiarize.
- Don't use unlicensed or copyright material without permission.

# 20

## SOFTWARE TOOLS

I f you are unsure about your writing, one of the best things you can do is use a software tool the give your text a once over and make suggestions for improvement.

### Spelling Check

The most obvious of these is the spelling checker, which I also talked about in the chapter *Proofreading and Editing*. There'll be a spelling and grammar checker built into the writing program you use, whether it's Microsoft Word, Apple Pages, Scrivener, BBEdit, or whatever. If you don't do a spell check before finalizing your doc, you're being negligent and disrespectful of your reader. Havin a heap o' spllng erors in yer text comess acruss like u just don give a durn.

Do you need to spell-check *everything*? Probably not. If you're writing an email to your mother, you can probably skip this step. (Mind you, I don't know your mom. She might be scary when it comes to that kind of thing.) But if you're writing an email to your CIO? I sure as heck would.

**Writing Aids**

Looking beyond the built-in spelling checker, there are tools that do a deeper dive into your writing and make more profound suggestions. The most popular of these are ProWritingAid (the one I use) and Grammarly (probably the most widely used). Many of them integrate with the tools you use, like your browser for when you're using Gmail, WordPress, or Facebook. They also have desktop clients, which means you don't have to be online to use them.

There are others too, both free and paid. Your employer might even have a site license for one. It's worth asking.

In the chapter *Proofreading and Editing*, I mentioned that I get Siri to read my text to me to find "the stupids." I also always do a pass using ProWritingAid for the same reason. This kind of tool is really good at finding things like:

- repeated words, where I've accidentally typed "and and" or "the the"
- instances of curly quotes facing the wrong way. "This sentence starts with the first curly wrong. It is an ending curly quote, not a beginning one."
- places to use active voice instead of passive
- extraneous, commas,
- double periods..
- weird grammar boo-boos that the spelling check missed.

Almost all of the paid tools have a free tier that lets you use the tool for short bits of text, then charges if you want to use it more, or more conveniently. ProWritingAid, for example, has a browser-based version that you can just type or paste text into.

So check them out. Like I said, ProWritingAid and Grammarly are the most commonly used, but if you search for "alternatives to Grammarly" or "free alternatives to Grammarly," you'll find many others to explore.

**Exercise: Software Tools**

Go to the website for the following tools, and try them out.

- ProWritingAid
- Grammarly
- Sudowrite
- Quillbot

# 21

# CHATGPT AND GENERATIVE AI

This chapter is the one I'm most nervous about, because it will almost certainly be out of date twenty seconds after I hit that big, red Publish button. I've rewritten it about a dozen times already. A year from now, this chapter might provide everyone a good chuckle.

Or maybe I'll be spot on. (I suspect I will be.)

As I write, generative artificial intelligence (AI) is having a moment. And it looks to be a Big Effing Deal.

As I write this sentence in (*glances at calendar*) ~~February~~ ~~March~~ April 2023, ChatGPT has been out for about four months, and has taken the world, especially the tech world, by storm. Rightly so. It's a sensation.

As of February 2023, 30 million people had already signed up for ChatGPT, and it had 5 million daily active users. It took Instagram, by comparison, a year to reach 10 million users, and that was considered explosive growth. Google, Facebook, and a host of other companies have already announced or launched competitors, and Microsoft has paid $10 billion to be able to incorporate ChatGPT into its Bing search, which is in beta as I'm writing this. A count of articles containing the term "ChatGPT" in my RSS reader (yes, I still use one of those) in the past few months revealed hundreds and hundreds of them just in the feeds I follow, and they ranged from the serious to the parody.

I asked ChatGPT, "What is ChatGPT?" Here's its response using the GPT-3 version of the software:

> "ChatGPT is an AI language model developed by OpenAI. It was trained on a large corpus of text data to generate human-like responses to a given prompt, allowing it to hold conversations with people and answer their questions."[1]

You'll often hear these tools referred to as Large Language Models or LLMs.

Obviously, I can't say what things will be like when you're reading this, but here's what I predict: the world, especially the world of text, will never be the same.

Perhaps you remember Clippy from Microsoft Office. It was a somewhat obtrusive software assistant (an allegedly "intelligent" one) built into the Office suite that tried to help with various tasks, like writing letters.

People hated Clippy.

*I* hated Clippy.

Deeply.

Why? Because it was annoying, obtrusive, and not very helpful.

But imagine a version of Clippy, only not so tiresome, and actually helpful.

That's where we're heading with ChatGPT and similar AI-based text tools. Tech giants and smaller companies alike are all working on different versions of them. They have some fantastic uses. If you haven't played with one, it's worth taking a few minutes to do so.

You can type in a prompt like, "What topics should a short, practical book on technical writing include?" and it will give a very reasonable list. That's useful. The AI (at the moment, anyway) couldn't write this book. It certainly couldn't express things with the panache and style that I do.

But for interrogating a topic? Generating ideas? Asking for simple explanations, or getting it to explain a topic so that a high school student can understand it? Well, there's value there. A lot of it.

The thing is, you have to be careful how you use this kind of tool.

Currently, ChatGPT is terrible with providing answers that rely on numbers. Its training set is out of date, so it doesn't know anything after September 2021. When it is wrong, it is wrong with supreme confidence. I've heard it described as the world's worst mansplainer, which I thought was funny. I've also heard it called the greatest bull-duster ever. (Okay, the person used a stronger version of that word). That's because the large language model it is built on is designed to create text that is plausible, not text that is accurate or truthful. I've heard it called a fancy version of the autocomplete you get on your phone. I've heard it called nothing but a gussied-up plagiarist. I've heard it called dangerous. I've heard it called a savior. The version built into the beta version of Bing went to some very weird places when it was first being widely tested, although they quickly reined it in.

It's been interesting.

Sometimes ChatGPT is like having a bright fifth-grader helping you out — capable, but not a lot of worldly context or experience. The tools don't do well with jokes or sarcasm. And, of course, there are copyright issues that have to be dealt with.

But sometimes it's like having a smart college student helping you out, and when it pops out something interesting, you can tell just how big generative AI is going to be in the coming years.

As a point of departure, it's very, very useful.

And it is only going to get better — and fast. Like I say, I worry this chapter is already outdated. For example, while I was writing this book, OpenAI released the GPT-4 version of ChatGPT. This is how it responded to my question, "What is ChatGPT?":

> "ChatGPT is an AI language model developed by OpenAI, based on the Generative Pre-trained Transformer (GPT) architecture. As a descendant of the GPT series, ChatGPT has been trained on a vast corpus of text data and leverages advanced machine learning techniques to generate human-like responses in a conversational context. It can understand and respond to various queries, create content such as poems or articles, and assist users in numerous tasks.
>
> As an AI-powered conversational agent, ChatGPT is designed to provide relevant and coherent responses in natural language, making it valuable for a wide range of applications, from customer support to content creation and beyond. However, it is essential to note that ChatGPT, like other AI language models, may have limitations in understanding and generating completely accurate or contextually appropriate responses all the time."[2]

You can see how much better the quality of that answer is.

I've tested the tool with all kinds of prompts. I gave it one that was similar to this: "Use the *Save the Cat! Writes a Novel* method to plot the 15 beats of an epic fantasy novel about an apprenticed dragon rider and his older sister, the head of the corrupt Dragon Riders' Guild. Include the apprentice's fiancée, who is also a dragon rider." What it produced was reasonably credible, and got better with questions that refined the idea. I'd still have to shape the story and write the book, but it was an interesting starting point.

On a more technological slant, you can ask things like, "Explain Agile software development as it applies to mainframe systems," or "List the features of an effective high-level structural design document." Again, don't take the results as gospel. ChatGPT itself will tell you it doesn't know if it is right or wrong, and suggests that you corroborate what it says elsewhere. But the tool can certainly point you in the right direction.

You can also give it text and ask it to improve it. Or give it a code snippet and ask it to help you find your mistakes.

I know there are teachers who are already using ChatGPT as a learning aid in their English classrooms. (But there are also schools banning it altogether. So there's that.)

A caution: make sure you don't break confidentiality or corporate policy by uploading something to the AI tools that you shouldn't. For example, the Very Large Government Department I worked for is, as I write, incorporating ChatGPT into the tools available to staff, but they won't be able to put anything into it that has a security classification of Protected or higher.

Will the tool replace you as a writer? No, I don't think so. You're still going to need to say things your way. But it can act as a handy assistant, and if writing isn't your strong suit, you may find that it can help carry you across the finish line and take care of some of the drudgery along the way.

I really do think these kinds of generative text tools will have a lasting, generally positive effect on corporate and technical communication. In fact, let me go further: I think we're at an inflection point. AI tools like this will change the world the way mobile computing did, and the way the internet did before that. I strongly suggest that you keep your eye on how these tools are developing. They're cool, and they're only going to get better.

But, like I said, be careful.

I'll leave the topic with this. I asked ChatGPT to give me a poem about Clippy, but in iambic pentameter.

Here's the result from the GPT-3 version of ChatGPT:

*Once, in Office suite, there lived a clip*

*Whose function was to aid with word and script*

*But oft his help was more a hindrance, rip*

*Than aid, and caused more trouble than it fixed*

*His paperclip form, with eyes so bright and bold*

*Invited users to click and seek his aid*

*But then he'd speak, with words both new and old*

*And leave one's work in disarray and cascade*

*His constant pop-ups drove the users mad*

*As they tried to work and Clippy would impede*

*His presence was a constant, nagging bad*

*And many wished that he would take the lead*

*But still, in spite of all the grief he caused*

*His memory lives on, an Office pause.*

*Cough* Shakespeare it isn't.

Here's the result from the GPT-4 version of ChatGPT:

*In cyberspace where digital realms collide,*

*A helper dwelt, in pixels he'd reside.*

*As Microsoft did forge the Clippy sprite,*

*He came to be, a guide amidst the night.*

*A paperclip, his form so plain, so true,*

*He offered aid to those who sought to do.*

*With cheerful smile and ceaseless, blinking eye,*

*He graced the screen, in Office did he lie.*

*"What might you need?" he'd ask with keen intent,*

*To ease the burden, oft his goal was bent,*

*In Word, Excel, or PowerPoint he'd dwell,*

*To guide and serve, his purpose to compel.*

*Yet, many cursed his visage, oft maligned,*

*His eager aid, to some, a wretched grind.*

*But Clippy bore the scorn with earnest grace,*

*His mission clear, to help in cyberspace.*

*Through versions past, his legacy remains,*

*As Clippy rests, no longer bearing chains.*

*His time has passed, but memories endure,*

*Of Microsoft's brave aide, forever pure.*[3]

You can see the improvement from generation to generation. And things are only going to get more impressive as the models improve.[4]

∽

**Exercise: Generative AI**

Choose a generative AI tool and play with it to see what it can do. You can use ChatGPT for free by signing up for it, but there are others out there, and there will no doubt be more available by the time you're reading this.

Try some of these as prompts.

- Explain cell mitosis as if I was a sixth-grader.
- Explain cell mitosis as if I was a high school senior.
- Explain cell mitosis as if I was a professional biologist.
- What's a good recipe for vegan tabouleh?
- What does "perihelion" mean?

And some techy ones, which, of course, were provided by ChatGPT:

- What are the key differences between various programming languages, such as Python, Java, and C++? Which language is best suited for specific tasks or industries?
- Can you explain the concept of containerization in software development, and how tools like Docker and Kubernetes help developers deploy and manage applications more efficiently?
- What is the role of machine learning in cybersecurity, and how are artificial intelligence algorithms being used to detect and prevent cyberattacks?
- How do blockchain technology and distributed ledger systems work? What are some real-world applications and potential benefits of using blockchain technology across various industries?
- What are the main differences between different types of databases, such as relational databases (e.g. MySQL, PostgreSQL) and NoSQL databases (e.g. MongoDB,

Cassandra)? How do these databases handle data storage and retrieval differently?

# 22

# STYLE GUIDES

A style guide is a document that describes standards for writing, formatting, and designing documents. It serves as a writer's and editor's reference to help create consistency and clarity in written materials.

Style guides can be super handy. These days, they're usually online, but you can still find them as books, as well.

Find out if your organization has one. The bigger your department, agency, or company is, the more likely it is that someone has taken the time to create one.

If so, this is a good thing. Use it.

What does a style guide cover?

Lots.

For example:

- **Terms and words.** Gives definitions for key terms and outlines the appropriate use of words and phrases, including industry-specific terms.

- **Formatting and layout.** Details how to format and lay out a document. It covers things like page layout standards, fonts to use, and how headings, lists, and tables are treated.
- **Voice.** Guides the tone used in the organization's writing. This might be formal or informal, serious or lighthearted — that kind of thing.
- **Grammar.** Lists the organization's punctuation, spelling, and capitalization preferences, and other elements of grammar mechanics.
- **Naming.** Provides naming conventions for files, folders, sections, and parts of a document.
- **Citations.** Gives standards for citing sources, whether in references, footnotes, or a bibliography.
- **Examples.** Gives examples of writing that follows the preferred style, showing headings, lists, tables, captions, footnotes, and other commonly used elements.
- **Glossary.** Defines key concepts used in the style guide. This is different to the terms and words section, which covers terms used by the industry.

The Very Large Government Agency I spent years working for had a style guide that they updated every couple of years. It was fifty-plus pages, and covered everything from when to use italics to the difference between hyphens and dashes, from number styles to how to cite quoted material, and from how to write inclusively (that is, not using words or phrases that reflect prejudice, stereotypes, or discriminatory views) to when to use capital letters when referring to a department or the government.

It wasn't riveting reading, but I often referred to it as the source of truth for how the Department wanted things written.

In fact, the Very Large Government Agency had:

- a writing style guide
- a quick reference style guide, that gave highlights

- a style guide specific to ministerial correspondence
- a branding identity guideline, which helped you figure out things like which logo to use and when
- a template for correspondence.

Your organization may have similar documents. Ask for them, or look them up on your intranet.

If they don't, there are other options. There are widely used, well-known style guides that you can adopt. (I mentioned some of these in the chapter *Numbers*.)

Commonly used style guides include:

- *Chicago Manual of Style*, which is used in the publishing industry and academic writing
- *Publication Manual of the American Psychological Association*, usually referred to as the APA, and used for a lot of writing in social sciences
- *Associated Press Stylebook*, which a lot people in journalism and media use
- *Modern Language Handbook*, usually referred to as the MLA and used a lot in the humanities, cultural studies, and liberal arts fields
- *IEEE Editorial Style Manual*, used by the Institute of Electrical and Electronics Engineers (IEEE) for its journals, conference proceedings, and standards
- *Microsoft Writing Style Guide*, a guide to writing style and terminology writing about computer technology
- *University of Oxford Style Guide*, which has a UK-orientation
- *Australian Government Style Manual*, the official style guide for the Australian government.

There are, of course, many others.

I don't particularly recommend one or the another. Which you should choose depends on what you're doing and who you're doing it for. Check them out and see which works for you. As with other advice in this book, being consistent is as the most important thing.

~

**Exercise: Style Guides**

1. Determine if your organization has a style guide (or more than one). If so, download it (or them), and read through them. Make notes on things you find useful, and items you were unaware of that you need to incorporate into your writing.
2. Check out three of the style guides mentioned in this chapter. Get to know them a little, and see if you can find points where they're similar and different.
3. Choose a style guide, either from your organization or one of the standard ones, and rewrite one of your documents so it meets the requirements of that guide.

# A FINAL WORD: ACCEPT IMPERFECTION

Here's the simple truth about tech and business writing: mistakes will happen. We are only human. It's no surprise that we sometimes flub a comma or use "effect" when we mean "affect."

Have you ever seen a mistake in a book by one of your favorite authors? (For that matter, have you found one in this book?[1]) It happens all the time.

A book, especially from a big publisher, usually goes through a rigorous, multi-phase editorial process before it's sent to the printer. It's a careful process that involves many people, all of whom try to weed out errors.

And yet, mistakes slip through.

In my own writing (both fiction and non-fiction), I have at least five alpha and beta readers, an editor, and a proofreader, who all go through the manuscript before I publish. And still, inevitably, my mom finds a couple of things that need changing once the book is out. (Thanks, Mom. I really do appreciate it.)

My point: try to do your best, and accept that mistakes happen. And when they do, correct them, and again, try to do your best the next time.

Remember, done is better than perfect. That applies to your writing as well. At some point, good enough is good enough. Write what you need to write, make it as good as you can, then put it out there.

~

Thank you for reading *Tech Writing Tips*. I have a bonus resource for you — *The Ultimate Tech Writing Review Checklist*. It's the perfect thing to have at your side when you've finished writing a technical document.

This two-page checklist will help you make sure you've thought about what you need to think about, and covered all your bases.

To claim your free copy, scan the QR code below.

# APPENDIX: EXERCISE ANSWERS

**Exercise: Answering the Two Questions**

There were three suggested topics for this exercise. I've given sample answers, but obviously, yours will be different.

What to do for this year's holiday party.

- Who's the audience? Everyone in my section, or on my team, or whatever group will be having the holiday party together.
- What do they need to know? The party will be on the last Friday in November. The party organizers are looking for ideas that can go ahead regardless of weather and won't cost more than $30 per person.

The refrigerator is being cleaned on Friday.

- Who's the audience? Everyone on the floor who shares the common refrigerator.

- What do they need to know? At 2 p.m., the fridge will be cleaned. Everyone needs to get their stuff out of it. Anything remaining will be thrown away.

The organization is instituting a One Computing Device Per Person Policy.

- Who's the audience? Everyone in the organization.
- What do they need to know? The one-computing-device policy is a cost-containment measure. Each person can have a laptop or a desktop, but not both. The Hardware Team will contact everyone known to have more than one device to discuss reclaiming the surplus. Exceptions must be approved by the CIO.

∿

### Exercise: What I'm Trying to Say

There were three methods discussed in the chapter (text, dot points, and mind mapping).

I've used a different method to answer each of them. Again, your answers will vary.

### What to do for this year's holiday party

*What I'm trying to say is that we're looking for ideas for the end-of-year holiday party. We don't want to do the same boring thing that we've been doing for years — going to a restaurant. This year we want to do something more active, like bowling, archery, or making glass art (or something like that). We'll still do a meal afterward. Whatever ideas people put forward, they need to be inexpensive ($30 maybe) so it isn't a burden for people. People can do either the activity, the meal, or both, but we'll need to know in advance so we can plan.*

## The refrigerator is being cleaned on Friday

*What I'm trying to say is:*

- *The fridge is a disgusting mess.*
- *We're hiring a professional cleaner to give it a solid cleaning.*
- *There's stuff that's been in there for months, if not years. Some of it is clearly never going to be used again.*
- *Everyone needs to get their personal items out of the fridge by noon on Friday.*
- *Anything that's left is going to get chucked out, regardless of whether it is labelled or not.*
- *If everyone can plan to have their stuff out of there by COB Thursday, that would be helpful.*

## The organization is instituting a One Computing Device Per Person Policy

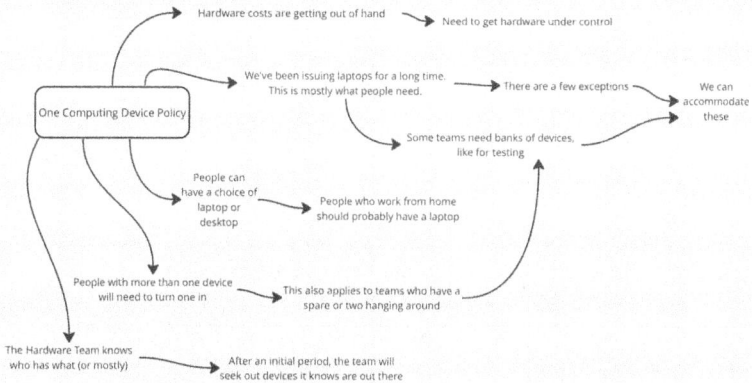

One Computing Device Policy

Hardware costs are getting out of hand → Need to get hardware under control

We've been issuing laptops for a long time. This is mostly what people need. → There are a few exceptions → We can accommodate these

Some teams need banks of devices, like for testing

People can have a choice of laptop or desktop → People who work from home should probably have a laptop

People with more than one device will need to turn one in → This also applies to teams who have a spare or two hanging around

The Hardware Team knows who has what (or mostly) → After an initial period, the team will seek out devices it knows are out there

∾

**Exercise: Rewriting in Active Voice**

Here are the passive sentences rewritten in active voice.

1. *The data will be encrypted by the server before it is transmitted to the client.*

Active: The server will encrypt the data before transmitting it to the client.

2. *The application is being developed by the team using the latest software development methodologies.*

Active: The team is using the latest software development methodologies to develop the application.

3. *The issue was fixed by the developer after several hours of debugging and troubleshooting.*

Active: The developer fixed the issue after several hours of debugging and troubleshooting.

4. *The proposal will be reviewed by the project manager before it is presented to the stakeholders.*

Active: The project manager will review the proposal before it is presented to the stakeholders. (Note, I could say, "The project manager will review the proposal before presenting it to the stakeholders," but that shifts the meaning a little, as the original does not necessarily indicate that the project manager is the presenter.)

5. *The system was audited by the compliance team to ensure it meets the regulatory requirements.*

Active: The compliance team audited the system to ensure it meets the regulatory requirements.

6. *The data will be analyzed by the data scientist using machine-learning algorithms to identify patterns and trends.*

Active: The data scientist will analyze the data using machine-learning algorithms to identify patterns and trends.

7. *The network is being monitored by the security team to detect and prevent unauthorized access and attacks.*

Active: The security team is monitoring the network to detect and prevent unauthorized access and attacks.

8. *The algorithm was optimized by the researcher to reduce the computational complexity and improve the accuracy of the predictions.*

Active: The researcher optimized the algorithm to reduce the computational complexity and improve the accuracy of the predictions.

9. *The update is being tested by the QA team to ensure it does not introduce new bugs or issues.*

Active: The QA team is testing the update to ensure it does not introduce new bugs or issues.

10. *The report is being generated by the software and will be sent to the stakeholders for review and feedback.*

Active: The software is generating the report and will send it to the stakeholders for review and feedback.

11. *The project was completed by the team on time and on budget.*

Active: The team completed the project on time and on budget.

12. *The requirements will be gathered by the business analyst and documented in the project plan.*

Active: The business analyst will gather the requirements and document them in the project plan.

13. *The system failure is being investigated by the support team to determine the root cause and find a solution.*

Active: The support team is investigating the system failure to determine the root cause and find a solution.

14. *The data will be backed up by the cron job at regular intervals to prevent data loss.*

Active: The cron job will back up the data at regular intervals to prevent data loss.

15. *The application update was deployed by the operations team using automated deployment scripts and configurations.*

Active: The operations team deployed the application update using automated deployment scripts and configurations.

16. *The system will be upgraded by the IT team to version 6.3.1 of the operating system for improved security and performance.*

Active: The IT team will upgrade the operating system to version 6.3.1 for improved security and performance.

17. *The code is being reviewed by the senior developer to ensure it meets the coding standards and best practices.*

Active: The senior developer is reviewing the code to ensure it meets the coding standards and best practices.

18. *The feature will be implemented by the developer in the next software release.*

Active: The developer will implement the feature in the next software release.

19. *The object is instantiated by the constructor method and initialized with default values before being modified by the program logic.*

Active: The constructor method instantiates the object and initializes default values before the program logic modifies them.

20. *The exception was caught by the try-catch block and handled by the error management code to prevent a system crash.*

Active: The try-catch block caught the exception and the error management code handled it to prevent a system crash.

∾

## Exercise: Rewrite to Make More Concise

I've reproduced the sample paragraphs and put the rewrites below them so you can easily compare the two. Your rewrites will almost certainly be better.

## Sample 1

*The utilization of multiple, distinct components in a computer system can result in increased processing capacity and improved performance. This is due to the fact that when these components are integrated, their individual functionalities can be leveraged in a complementary manner, resulting in a more efficient and effective system overall. This is particularly important in complex computing environments, where a single component may not be capable of handling all of the required tasks on its own.*

## Sample 1 (rewritten)

Using distinct components in a computer system can increase processing capacity and improve performance through the integration of their individual capabilities. This is crucial in complex computing environments, where one component may not be enough to do everything.

## Sample 2

*When designing software applications, it is important to take into consideration a variety of factors that can impact performance and usability. This includes factors such as the user interface design, the programming language utilized, the underlying architecture of the application, and the hardware resources available. By carefully considering these factors, developers can create software that is both efficient and user-friendly.*

**Sample 2 (rewritten)**

Developers must consider many factors to create user-friendly software that performs well. This includes user interface design, choice of programming language, the application's architecture, and available hardware.

**Sample 3**

*The rapid advancement of technology has led to the development of increasingly sophisticated tools and techniques for data analysis. These tools are designed to help organizations make sense of large and complex datasets, allowing them to extract valuable insights and inform decision-making processes. By leveraging these tools, organizations can gain a competitive advantage in their respective industries and stay ahead of the curve.*

**Sample 3 (rewritten)**

Technological advances have produced sophisticated data analysis tools that help organizations extract insights from complex datasets and gain a competitive edge.

**Sample 4**

*The adoption of cloud computing has become increasingly popular in recent years, as organizations seek to leverage the scalability and flexibility offered by cloud-based services. Cloud computing enables organizations to access computing resources on-demand, rather than having to invest in and maintain their own infrastructure. This can lead to significant cost savings, as well as increased agility and responsiveness.*

**Sample 4 (rewritten)**

Organizations adopt cloud computing for scalability and flexibility, so they can access computing resources on-demand and achieve cost savings and increased agility without the associated maintenance burden.

**Sample 5**

*In order to protect sensitive data and ensure the security of computing systems, it is necessary to implement robust security protocols and procedures. This includes measures such as encryption, access controls, and regular system patches and updates to address known vulnerabilities. By taking a proactive approach to security, organizations can mitigate the risk of cyber attacks and protect themselves from potential threats.*

**Sample 5 (rewritten)**

Robust security protocols protect an organization's sensitive data and mitigate the risk of cyber attacks. Measures include encryption, access controls, and regular system patching and updates.

∽

**Exercise: Rewrite to Make More Concrete and Specific**

The following sentences are rewritten to make them concrete and specific.

1. *The software features a user-friendly interface.*

Concrete and specific: The software features a responsive, intuitive interface with clear navigation menus and step-by-step tutorials.

2. *The mobile phone has a long battery life.*

Concrete and specific: The mobile phone's 4,000 mAh battery provides up to ten hours of continuous use on a single charge.

3. *The server handles a large number of simultaneous requests.*

Concrete and specific: The server handles up to 10,000 simultaneous requests with a latency of less than 100 milliseconds.

4. *The programming language is efficient.*

Concrete and specific: The programming language has a runtime performance comparable to C++ and consumes 30% less memory than Java.

5. *The algorithm processes data quickly.*

Concrete and specific: The algorithm processes 1 terabyte of data in under 12 minutes, making it three times faster than competing algorithms.

6. *The API has a broad range of functionalities.*

Concrete and specific: The API offers over 50 endpoints, including data retrieval, authentication, and real-time analytics.

7. *The security software protects against numerous threats.*

Concrete and specific: The security software provides robust safeguards against malware, ransomware, phishing attacks, and DDoS assaults, with real-time threat detection and automated updates.

8. *The mobile app has many useful features.*

Concrete and specific: The mobile app includes GPS navigation, offline map access, personalized route suggestions, and real-time traffic updates.

9. *The database stores a significant amount of information and keeps it safe.*

Concrete and specific: The database stores up to 500 terabytes of data, with support for horizontal scaling and automatic backups every 24 hours.

10. *The project management tool is versatile.*

Concrete and specific: The project management tool offers Gantt charts, task dependencies, time tracking, and collaboration tools that let it adapt to different project management methodologies.

∽

**Exercise: Document Structure**

Here's my response to the document structure exercise. For my answer, I've chosen a high-level system design.

A high-level system design (HLSD) provides a broad overview of a system's architecture, focusing on the main components and their interactions without delving into implementation details. Key components of a high-level system design include:

- **System components:** The main components or modules of the system. These could include hardware, software, databases, and external systems or services that the system interacts with.
- **Component relationships:** The relationships and interactions between the system components, including data flow, control flow, and dependencies between components.
- **System architecture:** The overall architecture and organization of the system, such as client-server, layered, microservices, or event-driven architecture. This can include any architectural patterns or principles that guide the design, such as separation of concerns, modularity, or scalability.
- **Data models:** The high-level data structures and models used in the system, as well as any data storage or databases that will be used. This could include entity-relationship diagrams or class diagrams showing data organization.
- **Interface design:** The interfaces between components, including APIs, communication protocols, and data formats. This establishes a clear contract between different parts of the system and enables modularity.

- **System constraints:** Any constraints or limitations that affect the design, such as performance requirements, security considerations, resource limitations, or compliance requirements.
- **Non-functional requirements:** The high-level non-functional requirements, such as performance, reliability, security, maintainability, and usability. These requirements affect the overall system design and architecture.
- **Technology stack:** The main technologies, frameworks, libraries, or platforms used to build the system, including programming languages, database management systems, web servers, and middleware.
- **High-level system diagram:** A visual representation of the system design, using block diagrams, system context diagrams, or deployment diagrams. These help convey the overall structure and relationships between components.

∾

**Exercise: Organizing Information**

1. Rewrite the following sentence using dot points to make it more readable.

*The application, built on a microservices architecture, utilizes a combination of RESTful APIs for synchronous communication, message queues for asynchronous communication, and a service mesh to provide a uniform way to connect, secure, and manage traffic between services, ultimately enhancing the system's scalability, fault tolerance, and maintainability.*

**Rewritten**

The application uses a microservices architecture and different communication methods to achieve enhanced scalability, fault tolerance, and maintainability, specifically:

1. Synchronous communication: RESTful APIs
2. Asynchronous communication: Message queues
3. Service mesh for inter-service traffic management
4. Connection between services
5. Secure communication
6. Traffic control.

2. Rewrite the following sentence by adding white space to make it more readable.

*In recent years, containerization technology has gained significant traction in the software development industry, particularly in the context of deploying and managing microservices-based applications. Containerization allows developers to package applications, along with their dependencies, into lightweight, portable, and self-sufficient units known as containers. These containers can then be deployed across various environments with minimal modification, simplifying the development, testing, and deployment processes. Docker is one of the most popular containerization platforms, providing developers with a comprehensive set of tools and a rich ecosystem for managing containers. In conjunction with container orchestration platforms like Kubernetes, developers can efficiently manage container deployment, scaling, and networking. The combination of containerization and orchestration platforms promotes a more streamlined development process, enabling teams to rapidly deliver high-quality software while adhering to best practices for reliability, scalability, and maintainability.*

**Rewritten**

In recent years, containerization technology has gained significant traction in the software development industry, particularly in the context of deploying and managing microservices-based applications.

Containerization allows developers to package applications, along with their dependencies, into lightweight, portable, and self-sufficient units known as containers. These containers can then be deployed across various environments with minimal modification, simplifying the development, testing, and deployment processes.

Docker is one of the most popular containerization platforms, providing developers with a comprehensive set of tools and a rich ecosystem for managing containers. In conjunction with container orchestration platforms like Kubernetes, developers can efficiently manage container deployment, scaling, and networking.

The combination of containerization and orchestration platforms promotes a more streamlined development process, enabling teams to rapidly deliver high-quality software while adhering to best practices for reliability, scalability, and maintainability.

∾

**Exercise: Ordered vs. Unordered Lists (Numbers vs. Bullets)**

I've rewritten the sample paragraphs as either an ordered list or unordered list.

**Sample 1**

> *When selecting a database management system for your project, there are several factors to consider. You should take into account the scalability requirements, data consistency needs, query complexity, ease of maintenance, and the overall performance of the system. By evaluating these factors, you can make a more informed decision about which database management system is best suited for your project.*

**Rewritten**

> Consider the following factors when selecting a database management system for your project:

- scalability requirements
- data consistency needs
- query complexity
- ease of maintenance
- overall performance.

## Sample 2

*To set up a new virtual machine using VirtualBox, start by down-loading and installing the latest version of VirtualBox on your host machine. Next, open VirtualBox and click on the "New" button to create a new virtual machine. Then, choose the operating system and allocate the required RAM and storage. Finally, boot the virtual machine and complete the operating system installation process.*

## Rewritten

Follow these steps to set up a new virtual machine using VirtualBox:

1. Download and install the latest version of VirtualBox.
2. Open VirtualBox and click the "New" button.
3. Choose the operating system for the virtual machine.
4. Allocate the required RAM and storage.
5. Boot the virtual machine and complete the operating system installation.

## Sample 3

*Let's configure a new web server using Nginx. First, install Nginx on your server. Next, create a new server block configuration file for your domain. Then, edit the configuration file to specify the root directory, server name, and location blocks. After that, test the configuration for syntax errors and reload Nginx to apply the changes. Lastly, verify that the web server is serving your website correctly by accessing it through a web browser.*

## Rewritten

1. Install Nginx on your server.
2. Create a new server block configuration file for your domain.
3. Edit the configuration file (root directory, server name, location blocks).
4. Test the configuration for syntax errors.
5. Reload Nginx to apply the changes.
6. Verify the web server is serving your website correctly.

## Sample 4

*When evaluating different cloud service providers for your business, there are several key aspects to consider. Factors such as pricing, available services, global infrastructure, security features, and support options should all play a role in your decision-making process. By carefully assessing these aspects, you can select the most suitable cloud service provider for your specific needs.*

## Rewritten

When evaluating cloud service providers for your business, consider the following factors:

- pricing
- available services
- global infrastructure
- security features
- support options.

## Sample 5

*Implementing a successful Continuous Integration (CI) and Continuous Deployment (CD) pipeline requires integrating several tools and practices. You will need to set up version control, automate the build process, perform automated testing, handle deployment, and monitor your application's performance. By incorporating these elements, you can streamline your development process and improve the overall quality of your software.*

### Rewritten

Integrate the following tools and practices for a successful Continuous Integration (CI) and Continuous Deployment (CD) pipeline:

- version control
- automated build process
- automated testing
- deployment handling
- application performance monitoring.

## Sample 6

*To create a new Python virtual environment, ensure you have Python and pip installed on your system. Next, install the "virtualenv" package using pip. Create a new directory for your project and navigate to it in the terminal. After that, run the "virtualenv"' command to create a new virtual environment within the directory. Activate the virtual environment to start using it for your project.*

### Rewritten

Follow these steps to create a new Python virtual environment:

1. Ensure Python and pip are installed on your system.
2. Install the "virtualenv" package using pip.
3. Create a new directory for your project and navigate to it.
4. Run the "virtualenv" command to create a new virtual environment.
5. Activate the virtual environment.

∾

**Exercise: Oxford Commas**

Consider the sentences that follow, and write down how the Oxford comma changes the meaning of the sentence.

**Example 1**

a. The conference attendees included the team managers, Alice and Bob.

b. The conference attendees included the team managers, Alice, and Bob.

In (a) above, without the Oxford comma, the sentence is ambiguous. It could mean that Alice and Bob are team managers, and they are the two people attending, or it could mean that team managers, as well as Alice and Bob, attended.

However, in (b), with the Oxford comma after "Alice," it's clear that there are team managers attending, as well as both Alice and Bob.

**Example 2**

a. The bug was discovered by the quality assurance specialist, a hacker and a programmer.

b. The bug was discovered by the quality assurance specialist, a hacker, and a programmer.

In (a) above, without the Oxford comma, the sentence could be read that a single person in the role of quality assurance specialist found the bug, and that they are also a hacker and a programmer.

In (b), the Oxford comma makes it clear that the bug was discovered by three separate people: quality assurance specialist, a hacker, and a programmer.

**Example 3**

a. The software was developed by the lead engineer, a perfectionist and a workaholic.

b. The software was developed by the lead engineer, a perfectionist, and a workaholic.

In (a) above, without the Oxford comma, the sentence could be read that lead engineer developed the software by themselves, and that they are described as a perfectionist and a workaholic.

In (b), the Oxford comma makes it clear that the software was developed by three people: lead engineer, a perfectionist, and a workaholic.

❧

**Exercise: Acronyms**

Consider this sample paragraph:

The CPU processes data received from the RAM. When the data is processed, the GPU displays the result on the screen.

The HDD stores data, while the SSD is faster but has less storage capacity.

*1. Make a list of the acronyms in the document.*

- CPU
- RAM
- GPU
- HDD
- SSD

*2. Write out the meaning for each.*

- CPU: central processing unit
- RAM: random access memory
- GPU: graphics processing unit
- HDD: hard disk drive
- SSD: solid state drive

*3. Considering your audience, decide if each term can be assumed knowledge or not.*

If my audience is technically literate, then these could all be considered assumed knowledge. But if I was writing, say, an introductory text for people who don't know much about computers, then none of them would be.

*4. Considering your audience, decide if each term should be in a glossary for the document or not.*

This is the same as the above. If my audience is technically literate, then these probably would not go in my glossary, although, if I was being careful, then I would. But for my introductory text, then all of them would go in a glossary.

*5. Rewrite one or two paragraphs that include acronyms to properly introduce them.*

The central processing unit (CPU) processes data received from the random access memory (RAM). When the data is processed, the graphics processing unit (GPU) displays the result on the screen. The hard disk drive (HDD) stores data, while the solid state drive (SSD) is faster, but has less storage capacity.

~

**Exercise: Numbers**

The following sentences have been rewritten to improve how they use numbers.

1. *The three-D printer finished 7 models in 4 hours, and 5 more were left.*

The 3D printer finished seven models in four hours, and five more were left.

2. *6 developers completed ninety percent of the project, while the remaining ten% was done by a 7th developer.*

Six developers completed 90% of the project, while the remaining 10% was done by a seventh developer.

3. *30 servers handle 70% of the load, and the other 30% is distributed among 10 additional servers.*

Thirty servers handle 70% of the load, and the other 30% is distributed among ten additional servers.

4. *The ten terabyte hard drive has a seven thousand, two hundred RPM speed and two hundred fifty six MB of cache.*

The 10 terabyte hard drive has a 7,200 RPM speed and 256 MB cache.

5. *On 8th of September 2022, the software release included 6 major updates and 20 bug fixes.*

On September 8, 2022, the software release included six major updates and 20 bug fixes.

6. *The team has 5 data scientists, 3 software engineers, and 2 project managers.*

The team has five data scientists, three software engineers, and two project managers.

7. *70% of users prefer the mobile app, while 30% use the desktop version.*

Seventy percent of users prefer the mobile app, while 30% use the desktop version.

8. *There are 4 main operations supported by the API: create, read, update, and delete.*

There are four main operations supported by the API: create, read, update, and delete.

9. *5% of the devices failed the quality assurance test due to 2 critical issues.*

Five percent of the devices failed the quality assurance test due to two critical issues.

10. *3 main goals of the project are increasing performance, reducing costs by fifty percent, and improving user experience.*

Three main goals of the project are increasing performance, reducing costs by 50%, and improving user experience.

∿

### Exercise: Unnecessary Capitalization

The following paragraphs have their capitalization mistakes fixed.

### Example 1

*The software Development team used python for their new Web Application. They chose Flask as the Web Framework, and the Database management system was postgresql. the team used Git for Version Control, and they hosted the repository on Github. they used the Agile Methodology, including scrum for project Management.*

**Rewritten**

The software development team used Python for their new web application. They chose Flask as the web framework, and the database management system was PostgreSQL. The team used Git for version control, and they hosted the repository on GitHub. They used the Agile Methodology, including Scrum for project management.

**Example 2**

*the Network engineers were tasked with setting up a virtual Private Network (VPN) for Remote Employees. They selected the Openvpn protocol and configured the Firewall to allow connections on Port 1194. They also provided Step-By-Step Instructions to help employees install and configure the vpn Client software on their devices.*

**Rewritten**

The network engineers were tasked with setting up a virtual private network (VPN) for remote employees. They selected the OpenVPN protocol and configured the firewall to allow connections on port 1194. They also provided step-by-step instructions to help employees install and configure the VPN client software on their devices.

**Example 3**

*Machine-Learning algorithms, such as Decision Trees, K-Nearest Neighbors, and Support Vector Machines, were evaluated for the Data Analysis project. The Team used Python Libraries, like Scikit-Learn, Pandas, and Numpy, to process the Data and train the models. The Model with the best Accuracy was chosen for implementation in the Production environment.*

**Rewritten**

Machine-learning algorithms, such as decision trees, k-nearest neighbors, and support vector machines, were evaluated for the data analysis project. The team used Python libraries, like Scikit-Learn, Pandas, and NumPy, to process the data and train the models. The model with the best accuracy was chosen for implementation in the production environment.

∿

**Exercise: Jargon**

The following paragraphs are rewritten to remove jargon or introduce it appropriately, as well as simplify. I'm assuming my audience doesn't know any of the acronyms or jargon.

**Original**

*The application's back-end is implemented using a MEAN stack, which includes MongoDB, Express, Angular, and Node.js. The team decided to use this architecture due to its advantages in horizontal scalability and rapid development. Moreover, the application leverages RESTful APIs for the CRUD operations on the database.*

*The front-end of the application uses several advanced JavaScript frameworks, such as React, Redux, and GraphQL. These libraries enable the developers to create a highly responsive and maintainable user interface. Additionally, the front-end employs AJAX to asynchronously load data and update the UI without requiring a full page reload.*

**Rewritten**

The team implemented the application back-end using the MongoDB database system, the Express web application framework, the Angular front-end web platform, and the Node.js JavaScript runtime environment. They chose this architecture for its advantages in horizontal scalability (that is, its ability to handle increased load by adding more servers) and rapid development. Further, the application uses RESTful APIs — web services that rely on Representational State Transfer — for the database create, read, update, and delete operations.

The application front-end uses several advanced JavaScript frameworks, such as React (a library for building user interfaces), Redux (a library for managing application state), and GraphQL (a query language for APIs). These libraries let developers create a highly responsive and maintainable user interface. Also, the front-end employs AJAX (Asynchronous JavaScript and XML) to load data and update the user interface without requiring a full page reload.

∾

## Exercise: Similes and Metaphors

Below are a simile and a metaphor for each of the technical concepts.

### Example 1: Data encryption

Simile: Data encryption is like locking your valuable information in a secure vault.

Metaphor: Data encryption acts as a defensive digital shield, protecting sensitive information from unauthorized access.

### Example 2: Network latency

Simile: Network latency is like a traffic jam that slows down data flow.

Metaphor: Network latency is the bottleneck that limits the speed of data transmission.

**Example 3: Cloud computing**

Simile: Cloud computing is like renting a car when you need one, instead of buying a car to cover all your trips.

Metaphor: Cloud computing is the IT version of a Swiss Army knife, offering multiple tools and solutions for a range of tasks.

**Example 4: Load balancing**

Simile: Load balancing is like having multiple checkout lanes at a grocery store to efficiently handle checkout traffic.

Metaphor: Load balancing is the system's traffic cop, ensuring that the flow of server requests are evenly distributed and handled efficiently.

**Example 5: Machine learning**

Simile: Machine learning is like training a dog to perform tricks, gradually improving its abilities through repetition and reinforcement.

Metaphor: Machine learning is a kind of digital brain that adapts and learns from data to make better decisions over time.

**Example 6: Distributed systems**

Simile: Distributed systems are like deploying a team of workers, each performing their tasks at the same time to complete a project faster.

Metaphor: Distributed systems are a technological hive mind, with multiple components working in unison to contribute to a common outcome.

**Example 7: Cybersecurity**

Simile: Cybersecurity is like a series of locks and alarms protecting a valuable asset.

Metaphor: Cybersecurity is the digital fortress that safeguards sensitive data and systems from potential threats.

**Example 8: Data compression**

Simile: Data compression is like vacuum-packing clothes to save space in a suitcase.

Metaphor: Data compression is digital origami, folding and compacting information into a smaller form without losing its core structure.

∾

**Exercise: Proofreading and Editing**

Proofread and edit the following paragraphs, making any changes needed to fix errors and express ideas better.

**Original**

*The companys new app has a Modular Fesign, which makes it easier to maintain and scale up. This is particularly important because the app is expected to grow rapidly in the coming months. In the past, the team faced several issues due to an tightly-coupled architecture and they wanted to avoid repeating the same mistakes again.*

*One of the key features of the app is its Integration with various 3rd Party Tools. Such integrations include 2-factor authentication, geolocation services, and Cloud-based Storage. Integrating these services can be complex, but the team has extensive experience with similar projects and have developed a set of best practices for streamlining the integration process.*

**Rewritten**

The company's new app features a modular design, making it easier to maintain and scale. This is crucial, because we expect rapid growth in the coming months. Previously, the tightly coupled architecture caused numerous issues. The modular design should prevent similar mistakes in the future.

The app boasts key integrations with several third-party tools, including two-factor authentication, geolocation services, and cloud-based storage. While integrating these services was complex, the team's extensive experience with comparable projects helped them develop best practices for streamlining the process.

# NOTES

## The Hatred of Documenting

1. Leo Laporte, *MacBreak Weekly* Episode 770: "Poseidon's Laptop," 16 June 2021.

## 1. The Two Most Important Questions

1. Pro tip: If you know you have the potential for a "hair on fire" situation (say, what you're doing is mission critical or on-time critical), it's a good idea to have a one-pager already prepared, which can be updated at short notice and delivered to the CIO ASAP. That way, you avoid being caught out.

## 5. Active Voice

1. My old English teacher would have told me I should use the term "past participle" here, but I think that's unnecessarily complex.

## 9. Organizing and Formatting

1. It's OK if you don't use Word. All decent word processors have some variant on this.

## 11. Send Your Commas to Oxford

1. Truss, Lynn (2004). *Eats, Shoots & Leaves: The Zero Tolerance Approach to Punctuation*. New York: Gotham Books. p. 84.
2. "Oxford Comma Dispute Is Settled as Maine Drivers Get $5 Million," *New York Times*, February 9, 2018. https://www.nytimes.com/2018/02/09/us/oxford-comma-maine.html

## 12. Acronyms

1. OK, "never" is wrong here. But we'll get to that.
2. In practice, people used the obvious acronym anyway, but in any document I wrote, I followed the style guide preference.

## 13. Numbers

1. There's a *This Is Spinal Tap* joke to be had in here somewhere.

   Also, did you ever notice that the umlaut in "Spinal Tap" is — completely absurdly — over the "n?" My thanks to my brother for pointing that out and making my day.

## 19. Don't. Just Don't

1. Do you have something you'd add to this list? If so, drop me a note. Maybe I'll include it in a future version. Use andrew@andreweinspruch.com.
2. If you can't tell what this word is, drop me a line, and I'll tell you.

## 21. ChatGPT and Generative AI

1. I also asked ChatGPT, "Can I use that as a quote in a book?"

   It responded, "Yes, you can use the above statement as a quote in a book, provided that you give proper attribution to OpenAI as the source of the information. Additionally, it's good practice to check the usage guidelines and copyright policies of OpenAI to make sure you are using the information appropriately."

   It then gave me this citation to use:

   ChatGPT by OpenAI. "ChatGPT: AI Language Model by OpenAI." 2023.
2. ChatGPT by OpenAI. "ChatGPT: AI Language Model by OpenAI." 2023.
3. ChatGPT by OpenAI. "Ode to Microsoft Clippy." 2023.
4. I used ChatGPT to help me generate many of the exercises in this book. I edited them all, of course, but the tool was extremely useful for helping me work out what to say and how to say it, and then I took it from there.

## A Final Word: Accept Imperfection

1. If you found one here, please let me know about it. Drop me a note at andrew@andreweinspruch.com.

# THANK YOU

Thank you again for reading *Tech Writing Tips*. Reviews are crucial for helping other readers discover new books to enjoy. If you want to help other technically-minded people find this book, please leave a review on the site of your choice. I'd really appreciate it.

Recommending my work to others is also a huge help. Feel free to give this book a shout-out to your colleagues and friends to spread the word. Many thanks!

# ACKNOWLEDGMENTS

It is a joy to get to say thank you to those who have helped me bring this book to the world.

Many, many thanks to my beta readers, Cheryl Hannah, Eric Einspruch, and Karen Lean, who all gave crucial input to the manuscript. Valuable and valued input all.

Thank you to my editor, Vanessa Lanaway, and my proofreader, Abigail Nathan. Sharp eyes and red pens, both. Y'all rock. It's that simple.

Thank you also to Edith Einspruch for casting final eyes on the text.

Thank you to 100 Covers for the fantastic cover.

A huge, massive thank you to my wife and partner, Billie Dean, and to our daughter, Tamsin Dean Einspruch, who both read and give fantastic input on everything I write. I love you both and I thank you.

And finally, thank you to you, whoever you are, for picking up this book and having a read. I appreciate it very much. May your words flow freely, and may your documents bring clarity.

# ABOUT THE AUTHOR

A.M. Einspruch has been a technical writer for well over 30 years, and has been involved with tech since the late 1970s, when he sold Apple II "microcomputers" for a small shop in Austin, TX called Computer 'n Things.

When he's not wearing his tech hat, he's wearing his author hat. His award-winning humorous fantasy series *The Western Lands and All That Really Matters* depicts a word of strangely specific weak magic, animals and humans who interact as equals, and wäÿ töö mänÿ ümläüts. Visit his web site for a complete list of his books at andreweinspruch.com.

Einspruch is an ex-pat Texan living in Australia, and is the co-founder of the not-for-profit charity the Deep Peace Trust (deep-peacetrust.com), which fosters deep peace and non-violence for all species. With his wife and daughter, he runs the Trust's farm animal and wild horse sanctuary. (You can see why there's the odd animal or two in his books.)

If pressed, he'll deny he ever coded in COBOL for a bank.

Click the links below to follow him on social media.

~

If you haven't done so yet, use the QR code below to claim your copy of *The Ultimate Tech Writing Review Checklist*. It's the perfect thing to have at your side when you've finished writing a technical document.

This two-page checklist will help you make sure you've thought about what you need to think about, and covered all your bases.